Endorsements

From the moment I read the first line, I was hooked. I have visited the ruins of the Seven Churches in Turkey and have been an avid student of Jewish history. Now, reading Revelation through genuine Jewish eyes is like watching TV in color for the first time.

I have studied Hebrew under Patrick for a number of years and I was delighted when he asked me to review and help edit this book. From the moment I read the first line, I was hooked. His Jewish roots and knowledge of the ancient customs, writings and beliefs lends incredible insight into the most mysterious of all Biblical writings. I have visited the ruins of the Seven Churches in Turkey and have been an avid student of Jewish history. Now reading Revelation through genuine Jewish eyes is like watching TV in color for the first time. I think you will be equally delighted with this work.

——Dr. Dale Robinson. Lay pastor who has led many tours to Israel, Jordan, Greece, Turkey.

I enjoyed reading R' Gavri'el's exposition of the book of Revelation. He skillfully expounds from a historical and traditional Jewish perspective. While there is much that can be unclear or unknown when trying to understand the Book of Revelation, R' Gavri'el presents a plausible explanation to some of its mysteries.

—R' Reuel Dillon, President of UMJA

For those who find Patrick Lumbroso's Hebraic devotionals as (kosher) food for the soul, you will find his new book on Revelation to be so much more. You may ask, "Why another book on this subject?" Most books emphasize predictions of the future based on symbolism. There are so many theories of what the future holds for this world. Lumbroso uses hermeneutics that are characteristic of classical Judaism which also uses the Tanakh: the Torah, the Prophets and the Writings. He does not shy away from using the stories of our respected Rabbis and Sages.

Patrick Lumbroso gives a fresh perspective on this mysterious and intriguing book. He shares his mastery of Hebrew and brings a new look at this prophetic book. I believe after reading this book, you will find not doom and gloom, but joy. It refocuses our perspective on the coming of His Kingdom on earth.

—Corey Sylvester, Messianic Rabbi of Temple Aviv Judea, Fullerton, California

Yochanan (John)

Presents the

Revelation

of

Yeshua the Messiah

A Messianic Commentary

BOOKS IN THE MESSIANIC COMMENTARY SERIES

MATTHEW PRESENTS YESHUA, KING MESSIAH

RABBI PAUL ENLIGHTENS THE
EPHESIANS
ON WALKING WITH MESSIAH YESHUA

JAMES THE JUST PRESENTS APPLICATIONS OF TORAH

JUDE ON FAITH AND THE
DESTRUCTIVE INFLUENCE OF HERESY

YOCHANAN (JOHN) PRESENTS THE
REVELATION OF YESHUA THE MESSIAH

PAUL PRESENTS TO THE
PHILIPPIANS
UNITY IN THE MESSIANIC COMMUNITY

JOHN'S THREE LETTERS
ON HOPE, LOVE AND COVENANT FIDELITY

YOCHANAN (JOHN)

Presents the

REVELATION

OF

YESHUA THE MESSIAH

A MESSIANIC COMMENTARY

RABBI GAVRIEL LUMBROSO

Lederer Books
An imprint of
Messianic Jewish Publishers
Clarksville, MD 21029

ISBN: 978-1-936716-93-7

2019 2

Library of Congress Control Number: 2018945402

Published by
Lederer Books
A division of
Messianic Jewish Publishers
6120 Day Long Lane
Clarksville, Maryland 21029

Distributed by
Messianic Jewish Resources Int'l.
www.messianicjewish.net
Individual and Trade Order line: 800-410-7647

Email: lederer@messianicjewish.net

Printed in the United States of America

ACKNOWLEDGEMENTS

This work could not have been written without my favorite critic, sounding board, cook, helper, encourager, promoter, fan, believer, and general-put-er-upper, my wife, Christina!

CONTENTS

General Editor's Preface

Nearly all bible commentators emphasize the importance of understanding the historical, cultural and grammatical aspects of any text of scripture. As has been said, "A text without a context is a pretext." In other words, to assume one can understand what God has revealed through those who present his word—prophets, poets, visionaries, apostles— without knowing the context is presumption. To really understand God's word, it's essential to know something about who wrote it and to whom, what was actually said and what it originally meant, when, where, and why it was written.

By now, everyone knows that the New Testament is a thoroughly Jewish book, written nearly entirely by Jews, taking place in and around Israel. The people written about—Paul, Peter, James, John, etc.—were almost all Jews who never abandoned their identities or people. The topics covered—sin, salvation, resurrection, Torah, Sabbath, how to "walk with God," the Millennium, etc.—were all Jewish topics that came from the Hebrew scripture. The expressions used often were Jewish idioms of that day. So, to fully understand the New Testament, it must be viewed through "Jewish eyes," meaning that the Jewish historical, cultural, grammatical must be examined.

There are commentaries for women, for men, for teens, even for children. There are commentaries that focus on financial issues in the bible. Others provide archaeological material. Some commentaries are topical. Others are the works of eminent men and women of God. But, until now, no commentary series has closely looked at the Jewish context of the New Testament books.

In this series, we have invited some of the top Messianic Jewish theologians in the world to contribute their knowledge and understanding. Each has written on a book (or more) of the New Testament they've specialized in, making sure to present the Jewish aspects—the original context—of each book. These works are not meant to be a verse-by-verse exegetical commentary. There are already many excellent ones available. But, these commentaries supplement what others lack, by virtue of the fact they focus on the Jewish aspects.

A number of different authors wrote these commentaries, each in his own style. Just as the Gospels were written by four different men, each with his own perspective and style, these volumes, too, have variations. We didn't want the writers to have to conform too much to any particular style guide, other than our basic one.

You may see some Hebrew expressions or Hebrew transliterations of the names in the New Testament. Thus, one writer might refer to the Apostle to the Gentiles as Paul. Another might write, Shaul, Paul's Hebrew name. Still, another might write Saul, an Anglicized version of Shaul. And some might write Saul/Paul, to reflect, not reject the different ways this servant of Messiah was known.

Another variation is the amount of reference material. Some have ample footnotes or endnotes, while others incorporate references within the text. Some don't have an enormous amount of notes, based on the book they are writing commentary for.

We have plans for a Messianic Jewish commentary series on the entire bible. Although much has been written on the books of the Hebrew Scriptures, and there have been some written by Messianic Jews, there hasn't been a full commentary series on the "Older" Testament. But, we hope to publish such a series in the near future.

So, I invite you to put on your Jewish glasses (if you're not Jewish) and take a look at the New Testament in a way that will truly open up new understanding for you, as you get to know the God of Israel and his Messiah better.

RABBI BARRY RUBIN
General Editor and Publisher

FOREWORD

With all the varying opinions about the book of Revelation, it is a blessing to finally have a book that will give us an understanding from a Messianic point of view, a point of view, that a Jewish person would understand hearing from God, living in that time period.

Having known Patrick Gabriel Lumbroso for over 10 years, I am continually amazed at how God uses him to communicate the truths of scripture from a Jewish perspective that is filled with the presence of the Messiah. In the three books that he has written, he has helped me to better understand the tremendous truths that are to be learned. He not only knows Hebrew but understands the Jewish world of the times of the New Covenant.

Whether it's writing or singing music with his wife Christine, teaching Hebrew or French or writing a book, you will find yourself understanding the Bible in a complete fresh and dynamic manner.

JOE GONZALEZ
Radio Station Manager and talk show host
Moody Radio

PREFACE

I warn everyone hearing the words of the prophecy in this book that if anyone adds to them, God will add to him the plagues written in this book. And if anyone takes anything away from the words in the book of this prophecy, God will take away his share in the Tree of Life and the holy city, as described in this book. (Rev 22:18–19)

These two statements that come at the end of the revelation Yochanan the disciple of Yeshua received on the Isle of Patmos represent a strong injunction against its alteration. To alter a text, one doesn't have to change words. A simple theological or chronological perspective can dramatically alter the meaning of a text, whereas changing a word can add to its clarity. The insertion of chapters and verses also contribute to giving us an understanding different from the original.

Thinking Jewishly about a Jewish text

Jewish Biblical writing is usually more thematic than chronological which sometimes can confuse Bible readers and leaves them guessing as to the chronology of events. I am fully aware of this regarding the text of the prophecy Yochanan received on the Isle of Patmos. I am also aware that some of the chapters as they are written in the text tell us about the same events, each time with more detail.

Also, much has been written about the Book of Revelation over the last of 2,000 years. And since the words received in this vision concern prophetic events, much of their interpretation has to be assumed, or guessed at, often using "circumstantial evidence" to unlock the meaning in a text.

As a Jew studying these writings, I have often felt uncomfortable with the fact that most of the assumptions concerning this prophecy are based on Christian "Replacement Theology," an idea that might have been conceived in the days of Yochanan but had not even budded, much less, birthed.

My first question was, "Since Christianity hadn't really been born at that time, why couldn't the Book of the Revelation be a Jewish book, understood through the texts of the Torah and its Jewish midrashic interpretations?" My next question was, "Why aren't Jewish interpretations at least part of this conversation?" As unconventional as it may seem, this book is an attempt to answer these questions..

To present the Book of Revelation from a Jewish perspective is a daunting task. It requires rethinking much of what has been written for two millennia. It feels to me a little bit like Copernicus who tried to convince people that the earth revolved around the sun at a time when most people were convinced that it was the other way around. I will therefore ask the reader to give it a charitable read and an honest hearing, patiently waiting for the "jury" to return. I know you'll find what I have written to be interesting and revelatory.

What This Book is Not

This book is not an attempt at an exegetical interpretation of the oracle Yochanan received on the isle of Patmos. It is neither an eschatological work designed to set a name and a date on every beast, bowl, horn, and shofar or any future events. My approach may open up this vision even more than many other commentaries on this esoteric book of the bible.

What This Book Is

This book uses true historical and cultural accounts in order to attempt to reconstruct how Yochanan, a Jewish follower of the Messiah, might have reacted to what he saw and heard. I also suggest that interpreting the Book of Revelation according to the Judaism in the days of Yochanan, instead of through different forms of Christianity over the centuries, will provide a new and perhaps more accurate approach to a correct interpretation of this often confusing letter.

About the Theme of This Book

People often view the Book of Revelation as about doom and disaster while forgetting that it represents the essence of the Good News of Messiah: the establishment of his Kingdom on earth. I compare it to a woman going through an extensive and difficult labor, who forgets all the pain at the arrival of the precious gift of new life she has just brought forth. It is my hope that in this work I will be able to restore the joy that comes from the anticipation of that coming day, not provide another dry, historical/theological writing using eschatological hermeneutics. I hope you will experience the happy ending coming from the fulfillment of the hope the Jewish people and all humanity have been waiting for, for so long—the establishment of God's kingdom in the earth.

As with many biblical texts, this prophecy has suffered from an identity hijacking. Most teachers interpret Revelation using theology from the eras of Roman Emperor Constantine, Martin Luther, or even modern rabbinical Judaism, none of which existed at that time. This is a grave anachronism. I say "grave" because it creates an alteration in the understanding of the text, which becomes an "adding to" or a "taking away" from it, against which, as we have just noted, there is strong injunction. Therefore, I endeavor to unwrap this oracle using theology pertaining to the classic Judaism of this era, the Judaism in which Yochanan (John) was raised. You'll read my ideas of what his thoughts were while pondering the words of Yeshua, who gave him the prophecy.

INTRODUCTION

The letter that is called The Book of Revelation was given to Yochanan in the same way other prophetic messages were given through prophets of old. As was once mentioned in the letter addressed to the first century Israeli believers, the only difference is the source:

> In days gone by, God spoke in many and varied ways to the fathers through the prophets. But now, in the acharit-hayamim [last days], he has spoken to us through his Son, to whom he has given ownership of everything and through whom he created the universe.[1]

This statement from the first century apostolic letter to the Messianic Jews in Israel (Hebrews) tells us something very important about the nature of contemporary prophecy. It clearly informs us that HaShem (lit. the Name, YHVH, the LORD), who up to that time spoke his prophecy through prophets, now speaks to us through his revealed Messiah. It states that whereas in times past HaShem spoke to the nation of Israel through national prophets, such as Isaiah, Jeremiah, Ezekiel, etc., he now gives his word to Israel (literally, the Jewish people), or "Greater" Israel (Jews + grafted-in Gentiles), through the Messiah of Israel, Yeshua.

At a minimum, this brings a certain distinction to the prophecy Yochanan received while he was exiled on the Isle of Patmos. Apart from this difference in protocol, like all other bona-fide prophecies, its purpose was mostly for guidance and encouragement to its contemporaries. And as with all other prophecies, it serves as a guide

1. Messianic Jews 1:1–2

and a blueprint to understand what the Tanakh and its traditional commentary, the Talmud, call the *acharit-hayamim*, the last days.

Who wrote this book, when and why?

The authorship of Revelation is reinforced in the first statement of the letter which, as with any important legal document, starts with an introduction to whom the letter is from, and of its intended purpose:

> This is the revelation which God gave to Yeshua the Messiah, so that he could show his servants what must happen very soon. He communicated it by sending his angel to his servant Yochanan, who bore witness to the Word of God and to the testimony of Yeshua the Messiah, as much as he saw. Blessed are the reader and hearers of the words of this prophecy, provided they obey the things written in it! For the time is near![2]

We now know from where the prophecy originated: HaShem gave it to Yeshua who communicated it to Yochanan at the end of the first century C.E.

We also know the goal of the prophecy: That HaShem's servant would know what must happen very soon.

The message also exhorts that its hearers are blessed by this prophetic message if, and only if, they obey the things written in it. Reading the prophetic message in this letter should have on us, today, what I call the "Josiah Effect." Here is what King Josiah said when he heard the words from the long-lost Torah:

> After the king had heard what was written in the scroll of the Torah, he tore his clothes. Then the king issued this order to Hilkiyah the cohen, Achikam the son of Shafan, `Akhbor the son of Mikhayah, Shafan the secretary and `Asayah the king's servant: "Go; and consult ADONAI for me, for the people and for all Y'hudah in regard to what is written in this scroll which has been found. For ADONAI must be furious at us, since our ancestors did not listen to the words

2. Rev 1:1-3

> written in this scroll and didn't do everything written there that concerns us."[3]

The blessing here, of course, is that having been warned, we now start applying ourselves to live the way we should. We "clean up our act" before Messiah comes. It's like a Jewish saying I heard one time: *Imah, Imah, maher, azor li lenakot et hacheder sheli, ki HaMashiach ba*! meaning, "Mother, Mother, quickly help me clean my room because Messiah's coming!" Ya'akov, the brother of the Master, taught this principle in these following words:

> Don't deceive yourselves by only hearing what the Word says but do it! For whoever hears the Word but doesn't do what it says is like someone who looks at his face in a mirror, who looks at himself, goes away and immediately forgets what he looks like. But if a person looks closely into the perfect Torah, which gives freedom, and continues, becoming not a forgetful hearer but a doer of the work it requires, then he will be blessed in what he does.[4]

In other words, what good is it to look at our reflection in a mirror if it is not to correct the wrongs we see in it?

3. 2 Kings 22:11-13
4. Jas 1:22–25

Chapter 1
A Heavenly Visitor

- Historical and Cultural Perspectives
- Social Background
- The Good News of The Kingdom
- HaShem in Exile with His People
- To the Angel of The Messianic Community in Ephesus …
- To the Angel of The Messianic Community in Smyrna …
- To the Angel of The Messianic Community in Pergamum ...
- To the Angel of The Messianic Community in Thyatira …
- To the Angel of the Messianic Community in Sardis …
- To the Angel of the Messianic Community in Philadelphia ...
- To the Angel of the Messianic Community in Laodicea ...
- Thoughts from the Author

Historical And Cultural Perspective

It all began in Ephesus, a city in Asia Minor, during the terror-filled reign of Emperor Domitian, between 81 and 96 C.E. (Common Era). Emperor Domitian had declared himself to be a god, and instituted that, along with worshipping him, people needed to also acknowledge him.

This of course did not sit very well with either the Jewish population of the day or with the Greek-citizens of the area who, through the teachings of Saul (Paul), instead responded to the Torah injunction:

> You are to have no other gods before me. You are not to make for yourselves a carved image or any kind of representation of anything in heaven above, on the earth beneath or in the water below the shoreline.[1]

These new believers and followers of Yeshua from the nations had rejected their local pantheon of gods to serve the one true God of the Jews, the One whom they recently discovered had created heaven and earth. They had joined themselves to the God of Israel through discipleship to the Master. Their challenge to Emperor Domitian's authority resulted in persecutions for their communities. The Domitian persecutions were the second set of persecutions. They were very short, but very severe. More than 40,000 people died.

It is at that time that Yochanan, Yeshua's beloved disciple, received this prophecy from the Master. Because the Romans had been unsuccessful in ridding themselves of Yochanan's annoying and challenging presence by attempting to boil him in oil, they exiled the irascible disciple to a labor camp on the Isle of Patmos.

I wonder if while in the boiling caldron, Yochanan remembered the famous words of the three Judean friends of the prophet Daniel while they themselves were in Nebuchadnezzar's fiery furnace:

> Our God, whom we serve, is able to save us, he will save us from the blazing hot furnace and from your power. But even if he doesn't, we want you to know, your Majesty, that we will neither serve your gods nor worship the gold statue which you have set up.[2]

We have no official record of such an event happening to Yochanan. But somehow the supposedly fatal process left the beloved disciple of the Master unhurt. We are therefore left to conclude that there must have been some sort of supernatural power protecting him, as there was in the case of the three Jewish friends of Daniel in the fiery furnace, who all came out, as Daniel reports, "without the smell of fire."[3]

1. Exod 20:3–4
2. Dan 3:17–18
3. Dan 3:27

Yochanan was, at that time, the last disciple alive who had personally listened to the Master. The destruction and burning of the Temple was still fresh in his memory. The following ancient Talmudic parable may have provided him with comfort:

> A father once prepared a beautiful suit of clothes for his son. But the child neglected his father's gift, and soon the suit was in tatters. The father gave the child a second suit of clothes; this one, too, was ruined by the child's carelessness. So, the father made a third suit. This time, however, he withholds it from his son. Occasionally, on special and opportune times, he shows the suit to the child, explaining that when the child learns to appreciate and properly care for the gift, it will be given to him. This induces the child to improve his behavior, until it gradually becomes second nature to him—at which time he will be worthy of his father's gift. (As told by chassidic master Rabbi Levi Yitzchak of Berdichev in his commentary on Talmud, Megillah 3a concerning Daniel 10:7.)

In the Jewish world, this parable was understood as concerning the rebuilding of the Jewish Temple. The records of the life of the beloved disciple show that he held such a strong faith in the ultimate victory of HaShem's purposes, that we can assume that in his mind, even if he died, the prophecies of the restoration of the glory of Israel and of its Temple would be fulfilled. Therefore, according to this parable, hope was in order. Apart from this parable, there was another reason why Yochanan should hope for (or look toward) the rebuilding of the Temple.

Over half a millennium prior to the burning and destruction of the second Jewish Temple by the Romans, a previous world power, Babylon, burned and destroyed the first Jewish Temple, built by Solomon.

After the Babylonians victory over Jerusalem, most of the people of the Judean nation were deported to the city of Babylon and its provinces until 70 years later, when the Medo-Persian Emperor Cyrus gave permission for all Jews in the Empire to return to their ancestral lands. He also provided timber and money for the rebuilding of Jerusalem's wall and for that of its Temple.

As the returned Jewish exiles busied themselves in rebuilding their Holy Place, it would have seemed natural for them to use the plan given to them through the prophet Ezekiel while in exile, but they did not. Why? Because the prophet's plans were different from the ones HaShem gave to King David. At that time, Ezekiel's Temple plans were frowned upon and Ezekiel was considered to be some sort of an anti-establishment religious rebel.

Because of this issue with the altered Temple plans, his revelations almost were not included in the prophetic canon, until a Jewish sage explained that the Temple Ezekiel prophesied about was not a post-Babylonian exile temple, but rather the Temple of the "World to Come": The Messianic Temple. It would make sense then, that as the second Temple was destroyed, hope would turn toward the third one: Ezekiel's Messianic Temple. Within this context, the destruction of Herod's temple becomes a source of hope that the Messianic Age truly is "at hand." Therefore, it must have been with great expectation and joy that, while on the Isle of Patmos, Yochanan received this vision of Yeshua within what seemed to look like the Temple.

Think of it! When it all seemed to have come to an end for everybody, the most wonderful thing happened. It was Fall. The season of the Fall Festivals of repentance and renewal, Rosh Hashanah, Yom Kippur, and Sukkot were at hand. As Yochanan was praying, the Master himself appeared to him from what seemed to be the Temple. Here is how Yochanan relates his dramatic experience:

> From: Yochanan To: The seven Messianic communities in the province of Asia: Grace and shalom to you from the One who is, who was and who is coming; from the sevenfold Spirit before his throne; and from Yeshua the Messiah.[4]

יוחנן לשבע הקהלות אשר באסיא חסד לכם ושלום מאת ההוה והיה
ויבוא ומאת שבעת הרוחות אשר לפני כסאו

4. Rev 1:4

In these first words, we have the introduction. Yochanan greets the seven Messianic congregations in Asia Minor in the name of "the One who is, who was and who is coming": Yeshua, and "from the seven spirits before his [Yeshua's] throne." These seven spirits usually refer to the seven archangels: Mikha'el, Gavri'el, Rafa'el, Uri'el, Suri'el, Fanu'el and Yechi'el, some of which we hear about in the prophecies left to us by Daniel. The introduction to the message continues in verse five with:

> … the faithful witness, the firstborn[5].

The firstborn, as in "first fruit", thus taking us to the Levitical laws of first fruits.

> … from the dead and the ruler of the earth's kings. To him, the one who loves us, who has freed us from our sins at the cost of his blood.[6]

These last words represent a beautiful encouragement to the persecuted Messianic communities who were risking their lives because of their faith in Yeshua. They were now reminded that this very same Yeshua has loved them so much that he gave his life to free them from corruption, as well as from the death of separation from HaShem. They were reminded that he still loved and cared for them in verse six:

> ...who has caused us to be a kingdom, that is, cohanim [priests] for God, his Father.[7]

Now the communities are being reminded of their very important Messianic roles in the world, which strongly define their destiny.[8]

The priesthood referred to here is a priesthood defined by the model of the only earthly priesthood allowed according to the Torah: the Levitical priesthood of the order of Aaron, the descendant of Levi, the son of Jacob/Israel. The tribe of Levi was set aside and not given

---

5. Rev 1:5
6. Rev 1:5
7. Rev 1:6
8. Mt 10:23–25; 2 Tim 3:12

tribal land in Israel so they could only serve HaShem. They were to be itinerant teachers to the rest of the tribes. In this sense, the Levites had to forego worldly ambitions and wealth. HaShem was their inheritance, not lands, not possessions.

The lifestyle of the priesthood sounds a lot like what Yeshua proposed to those who would choose to become his intimate disciples. In the 14th chapter of his chronicle on the life and words of Yeshua, Luke recounts a whole narrative about discipleship to Yeshua. He signs it with:

> So every one of you who doesn't renounce all that he has cannot be my talmid.[9]

The whole narrative that brings us to this statement certainly copies the Levitical priesthood model, which is to be understood as the lifestyle of the believers in the Diaspora. Through Yeshua's message, these disciples are being reminded that they are cohanim with a very high and privileged responsibility. As such, they have (or should have) renounced the ideas of wealth and personal ambition. Their only inheritance is HaShem so they are to live like those in the Qumran Essene community, the apocalyptic sect that abandoned Jerusalem and lived ascetic lives in the Judean desert, in protest against the way the Temple was being run. These words from the mouth of Yochanan almost sound like a pep-talk to encourage the troops, to remind them of the reason for their great calling.

It is the same today. If we are disciples of the Master, we are like cohanim. As Yeshua showed us HaShem's ways, we are to show Yeshua's ways to the world. That's what it means to be a cohen: to in some way represent the 'holiness,' the "set-apart-ness" being called by HaShem. Yochanan signs off this introduction with:

> ...to him be the glory and the rulership forever and ever. Amen.[10]

And now, for more encouragement, here is the pep-talk of all pep-talks (do you hear the heavenly cheerleaders?):

9. Lk 14:33
10. Rev 1:6

> Look! He is coming with the clouds![11] Every eye will see him, including those who pierced him; and all the tribes of the Land will mourn him.[12] Yes! Amen! "I am the Aleph and the Tav" [Hebrew equivalent for A to Z], says ADONAI, God of heaven's armies, the One who is, who was and who is coming.[13]

What an introduction! Yochanan continues:

> I, Yochanan, am a brother of yours and a fellow-sharer in the suffering, kingship and perseverance that come from being united with Yeshua. I had been exiled to the island called Patmos for having proclaimed the message of God and borne witness to Yeshua. I came to be, in the Spirit, on the Day of the Lord.[14]

The "Day of the Lord" refers to what is also called "That Great Day," or, Ba'Yom HaHu :ביום ההוא. the Day of the coming of the Lord at the end of the age.

Some believe that the events concerning Yeshua's return will take place during the Fall Festivals, which start with Yom Teruah, 'The Day of the Memorial of the Blowing of Trumpets' or, shofars, also known as Rosh HaShanah. It is a festival which reminds us of the sounds that introduced HaShem on Mt. Horeb.[15] Since the message Yochanan is about to receive takes us to the Day of the Lord at end of the age, he could have received this message at the beginning of the Fall Festivals:[16]

> And I heard behind me a loud voice, like a trumpet, saying, "Write down what you see on a scroll, and send it to the seven Messianic communities — Ephesus, Smyrna, Pergamum, Thyatira, Sardis, Philadelphia and Laodicea!"

11. Exod 19:6; Acts 1:9–11
12. Zech 12:10
13. Rev 1:7
14. Rev 1:9–10
15. Exod 19; Lev 23:24
16. 1 Thes 5:2

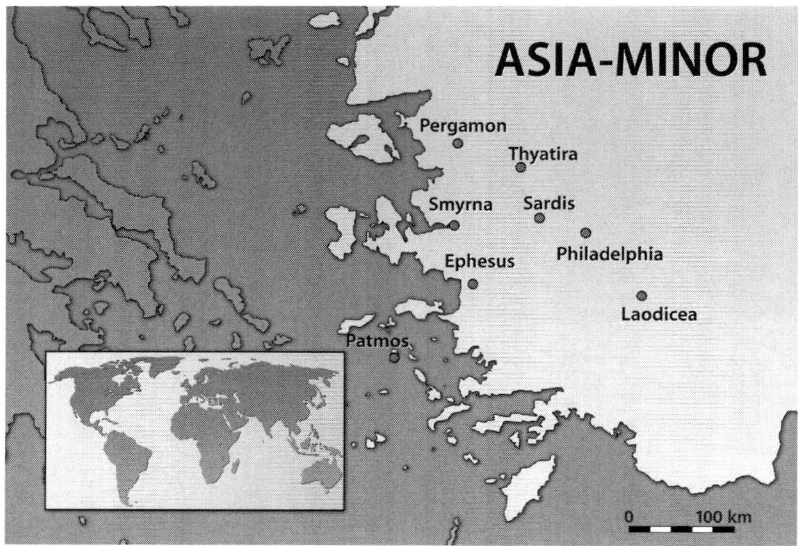

> I turned around to see who was speaking to me; and when I had turned, I saw seven gold menorahs; and among the menorahs was someone like a Son of Man...[17]

Yochanan saw a seven-branch lamp with his Master walking in the midst of it. Immediately, he must have remembered another prophet who had a similar vision:

> Then the angel that had been speaking with me [Zechariah] returned and roused me, as if he were waking someone up from being asleep, and asked me, "What do you see?" I answered, "I've been looking at a menorah; it's all of gold, with a bowl at its top, seven lamps on it, and seven tubes leading to the lamps at its top.[18]

The Torah never tells us what the golden menorah of the Temple represented. This allowed many of the give it various interpretations. One of the most common was that it represented the nation of Israel itself as a light to the worldYochanan therefore, had no problem

17. Rev 1:11–13
18. Rev 1:11–13

understanding that the seven lights of this menorah represented the messianic Kingdom of Israel in diaspora, each congregation being a branch.[19] He would later be warning one of these congregations: Therefore, remember where you were before you fell, turn from this sin, and do what you used to do before. Otherwise, I will come to you and remove your menorah from its place -- if you don't turn from your sin! (Rev 2:5)

> ...wearing a robe down to his feet and a gold band around his chest. His head and hair were as white as snow-white wool, his eyes like a fiery flame, his feet like burnished brass refined in a furnace, and his voice like the sound of rushing waters.[20]

Just like the prophets of old, Yochanan was asked to write down a message for the people. But who asked him? So far, the messenger in the vision has not been introduced. Even so, Yochanan was familiar with what he saw. The clothing described seemed to be a mix of the clothing of the High Priest, and that of a king of Israel. Yochanan, therefore, could not be mistaken in equating the vision with his beloved Master who appears to him as the High-Priest according to the order of Melchizedek.[21] Shim'on Kefa rightly said of the subjects of this priestly king:

> But you are a chosen people, the King's cohanim, a holy nation, a people for God to possess! Why? In order for you to declare the praises of the One who called you out of darkness into his wonderful light.[22]

Yochanan is now going to step into his role as a prophet. Jewish prophets did not typically get messages solely concerning the future. The definition of a prophet is given to us in the example of Aaron, Moshe's, Moses, brother:

---

19. Jewish New testament Commentary; David Stern page 792
20. Revelation 1:12-15
21. Gen 14:18–24; Ps 110; Heb 5:6
22. 1 Peter 2:9

> But ADONAI said to Moshe, "I have put you in the place of God to Pharaoh, and Aharon your brother will be your prophet."[23]

Like Aaron was for Moshe, a Jewish prophet speaks the words HaShem has for the people of their day. If these words happen to intersect with a future situation (which they often do), it is only a by-product of divine 'coincidence'. Like Aaron of old, Yochanan is now going to transcribe divine messages addressed to the seven congregations of Asia Minor, These words would be, as with the words of other prophets, for guidance and encouragement.

What would this message be?

If we consider their own history and understand the messages the Master gave Yochanan for them, we may be able to glean some useful advice for today. We have today true followers of Yeshua, who are subject to affliction because of their commitment to live in the Torah of the Master. How many throughout the centuries have been rejected by their families and their communities just because they found him who they believed was the Jewish messiah? How many Messianic Jews today in Israel face the possibility of being evicted from the Land of their fathers just because they have confessed to believing? How many believers suffer insults, disparagement and even physical persecution at the hand of ultra-orthodox Jews who still feel it is their duty to persecute those of the Way?[24] For them, this work may be more relevant than for those who presently don't suffer such afflictions. If you are part of the latter rather than the former, remember that if you are a true disciple, it might just come. Paul the shaliach tells us that:

> Indeed, all who want to live a godly life united with the Messiah Yeshua will be persecuted.[25]

To which, Shim'on Kefa adds:

> For the time has come for the judgment to begin. It begins with the household of God; and if it starts with us, what will the outcome be for those who are disobeying God's Good News?[26]

---

23. Exod 7:1
24. Acts 9:2
25. 2 Tim 3:12
26. 1 Pet 4:17

The answer to Shim'on's question lies in the prophetic vision Yeshua gave to Yochanan. Yochanan continued describing the vision:

> In his right hand he held seven stars, out of his mouth went a sharp double-edged sword, and his face was like the sun shining in full strength.[27]

Yochanan is very well versed in the prophetic texts. He knows that Abraham was promised, "I will most certainly bless you; and I will most certainly increase your descendants to as many as there are stars in the sky…"[28] Yochanan also remembers the prophecy from Isaiah, and knows it from the passage, "He has made my mouth like a sharp sword."[29]

> When I saw him, I fell down at his feet like a dead man.[30]

Just like Daniel, Ezekiel, and Jeremiah, Yochanan is awestruck by what he sees. Many people claim that HaShem speaks to them, but I see in these words what happens when the glory of the Almighty comes to speak with someone. It doesn't create a touchy-feely, warm-and-fuzzy sensation. From what I read in the book of Exodus and throughout the prophets, such events seem to leave their audience awestruck with fear and even sometimes unconscious. As with the other prophets though, a comforting hand and voice came to reassure the weakened human recipient. The "apparition" is followed with a formal introduction, which is again to be understood via Talmudic imagery:

> He placed his right hand upon me and said, "Don't be afraid! I am the First and the Last."[31]

27. Rev 1:16
28. Gen 22:17
29. Isa 49:2
30. Rev 1:17
31. Rev 1:17

HaShem introduced himself to Isaiah with those very same words[32]but here, Yeshua uses them to introduce himself. There is no difficulty here. In days of old, a king such as Achashverosh (see the book of Esther) gave his ring to Haman, so he could conduct business for him. The presence of this ring on Haman's finger said to the people of Babylon, "I am here in the name and authority of King Achashverosh. I represent him in all I do and say. I am he and he is me. He has given me all authority in the Kingdom and put all things under my feet. Achashverosh and I are one!" When Haman abused and misused that authority in using it to threaten HaShem's people, the ring was taken away from him and was given to Mordechai, who in turn used it to protect the Messianic seed. This story that we tell every year during the festival of Purim is the earthly replica of a cosmic play in the heavenly realms.

When HaSatan challenged Yeshua in the Judean desert, he said, "I will give you all this power and glory. It has been handed over to me, and I can give it to whomever I choose."[33] Like Haman, HaSatan carries authority over the earthly kingdom. But this enemy of all righteousness has used his power to attempt to destroy the Jewish Messianic seed. So this universal authority has been given to someone else who will use it to give life, not to kill. It is recorded that just before ascending to the Father, Yeshua said, "All authority in heaven and on earth has been given to me."[34] He has indeed been a worthy son and has earned the right and privilege to represent the Father, and therefore use his signet introduction, "I am the First and the Last."

The introduction continues. Yeshua knows that even to this day, many come in his name and pretend to be him. Some such as Simon Magus[35] even used magic, following the disciples everywhere they went to deceive the believers. So, as he gave his message to Yochanan, Yeshua wanted to make sure there was no confusion in

32. Isa 44:6; 48:12
33. Lu 4:6
34. Mt 28:18
35. Acts 8:9

Yochanan's mind as to who was talking to him, so he continues in verse eighteen with:

> ...the Living One. I was dead, but look! - I am alive forever and ever![36]

That does it. The disciples, along with 500 other people, were living testimonies of the actual resurrection of the Master. Now, Yochanan was sure!

> ... And I hold the keys to Death and Sh'ol.[37]

This was another identification piece. A key is an opening instrument. Yochanan, an avid Torah student, surely remembered Ezekiel's prophetic words, "Then you will know that I am ADONAI when I have opened your graves and made you get up out of your graves, my people!"[38]

Now that he fully identified himself both visually and verbally, Yeshua wants to give his messages to Yochanan to be shared with the Asian congregations. It is remarkable here to notice how much went into the identification, so that there would not be any mistake. Here are some of Yochanan's own thoughts on the subject:

> Beloved, believe not every spirit, but try the spirits whether they are of God: because many false prophets are gone out into the world.[39]

> So write down what you see, both what is now, and what will happen afterwards.[40]

Yochanan is to do what? This is important information if we want to understand the content of the text. He is to write what he sees:

> Now and
> What will happen afterwards

36. Rev 1:18
37. Rev 1:18
38. Ezek 3&:13
39. 1 John 4:1
40. Rev 1:19

The "now" part, of course, corresponds to his own time at the end of the first century C.E. The "afterwards" part corresponds to a time future to that of Yochanan's. Yeshua now will start unveiling the meaning of his cryptic apparition. He says:

> Here is the secret meaning of the seven stars you saw in my right hand, and of the seven gold menorahs: the seven stars are the angels of the seven Messianic communities, and the seven menorahs are the seven Messianic communities.[41]

Social Background

Now Yeshua uses Yochanan to communicate with the seven Messianic congregations around the Aegean Sea. These Messianic congregations included many non-Jewish members who came to Messianic Judaism through discipleship to the Master. These served alongside the Israeli believers, Messianic Jews practice Judaism with the awareness that Yeshua of Nazareth is the long-awaited, promised Messiah of the Jewish people and follow his teaching and life. He will in time establish the Kingdom of God on earth. In each of these Greek cities, the Greco-Roman Gentile disciples learned the Judaism of Yeshua by following in the footsteps of his Jewish disciples.

Where did these congregations come from? How did these Jewish disciples of Yeshua of Nazareth come to populate these local assemblies? Why did they even leave Israel?

These assemblies were born through the work of Paul and Barnabas in Asia Minor. Paul's background as an observant Jew born in the Gentile city of Tarsus made him a perfect tool to bring Messianic Judaism to this Mediterranean region. Not only was he well-versed in Jewish religion, culture, practices, and traditions, but he was very knowledgeable in Greek philosophy, religion, mores, and culture. By the time Paul was beheaded in Rome, he had left behind him a great legacy of followers of the Master, a legacy born through his exemplary dedication and lifestyle and nurtured through his letters.

41. Rev 1:20

To leave Israel to bring Messianic Judaism to the nations was something that Yeshua had commanded his disciples to do. Just before his ascension he said to them:

> All authority in heaven and on earth has been given to me. Therefore, go and make people from all nations into talmidim, immersing them into the reality of the Father, the Son and the Ruach HaKodesh, and teaching them to obey everything that I have commanded you. And remember! I will be with you always, yes, even until the end of the age.[42]

Mark relates the Master's ordinance in the following words:

> Then he said to them, "As you go throughout the world, proclaim the Good News to all creation."[43]

The Good News of The Kingdom

To truly define the social position of these disciples of the Rabbi from Nazareth, it is essential to understand what is meant by this 'Good News' they were to proclaim. In Hebrew, the word for "good news," is *Besorah* בשורה ευαγγελιον "euaggelion" in Greek, from which is derived our English word, "Gospel."

Today, if we are to understand Yeshua's command to his disciples concerning this *Besorah,* we must understand how they understood it then. To that end, we must find out what the word meant in the text of the Tanach. Considering the different instances where biblical prophets and writers used this expression, we find out that the 'Good News' refers to the time when the Jewish Messiah will reign over all the earth from a restored Jerusalem as the central spiritual and political nerve of civilization. At that time, all nations will be subject to the Jewish King, and even bring tribute to Jerusalem. In the days of Yochanan, the Roman Empire still gloated over its victory over Jerusalem. To acknowledge anyone but the Emperor as ruler was treason enough.

42. Mt 28:18–20
43. Mk 16:15

But all the more subversive and dangerous if that king is Yeshua from Nazareth, the itinerant rabbi who was executed by the Roman Empire. To proclaim that he resurrected and that he will eventually rule the world, including the Roman Empire, from Jerusalem as its glorious capital, was a very dangerous doctrine.

Now we can perhaps understand why the Israeli disciples were not so willing to leave the comfort and relative security of Israel to go to places where they were to proclaim such controversial ideas. Additionally, because these countries did not live by the biblical Jewish food requirements, nor its established festivals, for a Jewish disciple in the Diaspora, everything was complicated, even the weekly Shabbat observance. It actually took persecution in Israel to send them on their way. This persecution is related to us by Luke, Paul's faithful Macedonian scribe, biographer, doctor, and servant in the following words:

> It was around this time that King Herod began arresting and persecuting certain members of the Messianic community; and he had Ya`akov, Yochanan's brother, put to death by the sword. When Herod saw how much this pleased the Judeans, he went on to arrest Kefa as well. It was during the Days of Matzah.[44]

We can imagine that when that happened, the disciples' emotions must have been a mix of fear and of excitement. They could probably remember their dear Master's words saying:

> They will ban you from the synagogue; in fact, the time will come when anyone who kills you will think he is serving God![45]

It was already tough to be a follower of the Rabbi from Nazareth in Israel in the days preceding and following the destruction of the Temple in 70 C.E. But due to the intense Domitian persecutions, these Israeli believers who fled Israel to the Diaspora congregations might have felt that they were jumping from the frying pan into the fire.

---

44. Acts 12:1–3
45. Jn 16:2

We must remember here that these persecutions were mainly caused by the adherence of Yeshua's disciples, both Jews and Gentiles, to the first and second of the Ten Commandments, which represented an unbearable challenge to Domitian's self-claims of godhood.

Hashem in Exile with His People

As in days of old, HaShem heard the cry of his children. Through the medium of Yeshua's communications via Yochanan, he sent messages of encouragement, guidance, and warning to his people. When they received these messages, the Jewish disciples must have remembered the sage's teaching that "when HaShem sends his children in exile, he goes there with them" (Megilah 29a).

A story I once heard illustrates the idea. It is about a father who punished his boy for misbehaving at the dinner table. The father became so angry that he told the child to forego dinner and sent him to sleep in the attic. Later, this compassionate patriarch thought himself to have been a little harsh. When this father went to check on his son, he found him sleeping on the bare floor of the attic. What did the father do? He lay beside him all night, using his arm as a pillow for his son.

Our compassionate father, HaShem, always seems to be present in our afflictions in this manner. We read in English bibles that on Mt. Horeb, HaShem tells Moshe, "Go to Egypt…" but the Hebrew text says, "Come to Pharaoh." Why is he in Egypt? Here is what the text of Torah tells us:

> ADONAI said, "I have seen how my people are being oppressed in Egypt and heard their cry for release from their slavemasters, because I know their pain. I have come down to rescue them from the Egyptians and to bring them up out of that country to a good and spacious land, a land flowing with milk and honey, the place of the Kena`ani, Hitti, Emori, P'rizi, Hivi and Y'vusi. Yes, the cry of the people of Isra'el has come to me, and I have seen how terribly the Egyptians oppress them."[46]

46. Ex 3:7–9

HaShem sees the oppression his children are subjected to. He sees their tears. He hears their cries. He does not just loftily look down from above. He comes down to their rescue.

With this understanding and that of the 'Good News' according to the Tanach, we can imagine the surprise of Yochanan at the apparition of the Master on the Isle of Patmos. As in the days of Moshe, he probably felt that deliverance was at hand.

Therefore, the messages that Yeshua is about to deliver for his congregations around the Aegean Sea were a reinforcement of the fact that as with the children of Israel in the days of the Exodus, of the Judges, of Queen Esther, and of the Maccabees, they were not alone nor forsaken. It was to remind them that the Rock in which they trusted was dependable and available; that he did not fail. It was also to remind them that their destiny was part of the great cosmic plan of history.

The Jewish disciples were familiar with the stories of the Babylonian exile. They remembered how at that time, HaShem confirmed his presence with them through a slew of prophets. Some were in the land (Jeremiah); some in the provinces of Babylon (Ezekiel); and some were even in the palace of the Babylonian ruler (Daniel). Jeremiah, Ezekiel, and Daniel were in those days the main ministers of HaShem's words to give guidance and encouragement to his people in exile. As it was then, so it was in the narrative of HaShem's Diaspora children in the first century C.E. The Master's Jewish disciples became the ministers of HaShem's word for the congregations. Like the Israelites of old, they had lost all political, social, and economic clout in their society. So, the Jewish disciples taught their Greek brothers and sisters about the Exodus from Egypt, the Babylonian Exile, and about all the times that HaShem showed his mighty hand in favor of his people.

Of all the disciples of the Master, Yochanan was then the last one alive. He is on the Isle of Patmos, a forced labor camp for dissenters and political prisoners. What does HaShem want to tell his people? What can he tell them that would give them hope and guidance? It seems that today, just as it was at the time of Yochanan, we live in a world where it is becoming more and more controversial to live according to the tenets of the Torah as taught by our Master Yeshua. So, my question is this: do these messages have something relevant for us too?

His address to each of the seven congregations is tailored according to their geo-political, as well as economic realities. Should it seem strange that the agent of creation is able to connect with his congregations in such a manner? Just imagine yourself as one of these Gentile believers who has been grafted into the destiny of Israel through the agency of the King and Messiah of the Jews. As you hear these words, you now realize that HaShem, the foreign God of the Jews, knows you personally; he knows where you're from; he even knows the history of your city. The first message is to the city of Ephesus, the very city Yochanan shepherded.

To the Angel of the Messianic Community in Ephesus

Ephesus was the most important city of proconsular Asia. Situated at the mouth of the Cayster River, on a gulf of the Aegean Sea, it flourished as an important commercial and export center for Asia. In the days of Paul, it had grown to at least 250,000 people. From the Island of Patmos, Ephesus would be the first congregation you would meet. The nearest seaport to Patmos is Miletus,[47] which you would follow along the coast road to Ephesus. Ephesus also had its own important port, so you could go directly by ship from Patmos to Ephesus.

Paul established the congregation in Ephesus. He had a big impact on the Jewish community there. When he left, he designated Priscilla and Aquila as its overseers.[48] At a later time, Paul discovered that some disciples had not been immersed unto the Holy Spirit but only unto the immersion of Yochanan. But, when Sha'ul [Paul] placed his hands on them, the Ruach HaKodesh came upon them.[49]

47. Acts 20:15
48. Acts 18:19
49. Acts 19:6

Paul spoke in the Ephesus synagogue for three months (Acts 19:8) and then in the lecture hall of Tyrannus for two years.[50] In Ephesus, the making and selling of silver images to the fertility goddess Artemis was big business that brought wealth to the city. Therefore, Paul's teaching against idols created a disturbance among the merchants who feared that people would lose interest in the idols, which would then cause them to lose business. [51]

Paul wrote a long letter to the Ephesians' congregation. In his farewell to the elders of Ephesus at Miletus, before going to Jerusalem,[52] he warned them that savage wolves would come in among them.[53] This letter shows clearly that it was a mature congregation. It is also thought that Miriam, the mother of the Master, settled at Ephesus along with Yochanan who cared for her as per the Master's instructions.

> To the angel of the Messianic Community in Ephesus, write: 'Here is the message from the one who holds the seven stars in his right hand and walks among the seven gold menorahs.[54]

The introduction in Chapter One tells us that the stars are the angels of the congregations. The word angel or *mal'akh* מלאך in Hebrew is the same as the word "envoy." It is widely understood by scholars that these angels were actually the leaders of each congregation. Each congregation is represented by one menorah מנורה meaning "lamp," or referring to the seven-branched candelabrum. In any case, the introduction brings the comfort that each of the leaders is safely in the hands of the Master, and that he is present, walking among them.

> I know what you have been doing, how hard you have worked, how you have persevered, and how you can't stand wicked people; so you tested those who call themselves emissaries but aren't—and you found them to be liars. You are persevering, and you have suffered for my sake without growing weary.[55]

50. Acts 19;9–10
51. Acts 19:23
52. Acts 29:17–38
53. Acts 20:29
54. Rev 2:1
55. Rev 2:2–3

Yeshua is aware that the congregation needs encouragement. It must have been a big boost to their morale to realize that Yeshua, the Master himself, was aware of and concerned about them. He lets them know that he is aware of their efforts. It seems that just as Yeshua, Paul, and Peter had warned, the Ephesians had problems with self-appointed false teachers who claimed to be 'sent ones.' or sh'likhim of Yeshua but were not. In their ignorance of HaShem's ways, these people probably really thought they were sent by HaShem:

> But I have this against you: you have lost the love you had at first. Therefore, remember where you were before you fell, turn from this sin, and do what you used to do before. Otherwise, I will come to you and remove your menorah from its place — if you don't turn from your sin![56]

As we read the history of this congregation, we discover strong fervor and dedication. Miracles happen; the establishment is fearlessly challenged and people are forever changed as they leave behind the dead deeds of idolatry.[57] This part of Yeshua's message to Ephesus seems to carry the same tone as HaShem's message to Judah through the prophet Jeremiah about the nation's early devotion, I remember your devotion when you were young; how, as a bride, you loved me; how you followed me through the desert, through a land not sown[58], a message Yochanan was familiar with. Even in the tenderest of marriages, hot fervor can vanish in the routine of every day cares and life can become a matter of routine. The same phenomenon happens in the life of service to HaShem; but is he satisfied with our dutiful obedience? Is the observance of Shabbats and Festivals a chore and something we'd rather do without? Do they cramp our activities, lifestyles, and schedule? Do we bribe HaShem through works of charity? Or does fervor from a heart of loving gratitude motivate our service and obedience?

---

56. Rev 2:4–5
57. Eph 5:11
58. Jer 2:2

> But you have this in your favor: you hate what the Nicolaitans do — I hate it too. Those who have ears, let them hear what the Spirit is saying to the Messianic communities.[59]

HaShem now encourages his people, who hate the devious idolatrous and sexual practices of the Nicolaitans.[60] Yochanan knows this congregation. He is glad to send them some encouragement:

> To him winning the victory, I will give the right to eat from the Tree of Life which is in God's Gan-`Eden.[61]

This letter was not addressed to the people of the city of Ephesus as a whole. It was addressed to a group of people from Ephesus, a group composed of Jews and of Gentiles, who had acknowledged HaShem's supremacy in their lives. They knew that he was the God of Abraham, of Isaac, and of Jacob. They knew also that it is he who created the heavens and the earth. These people had already made the life-changing dangerous decision to serve HaShem through subjecting themselves to the discipleship of Yeshua as their Messiah. In spite of this, in this letter, they are told that their right to "eat from the Tree of Life, which is in Gan-Eden" was dependent on winning the victory. The question then that begs to be asked is, "What does 'win the victory' look like?" The answer to that question is the main message of this oracle that Yeshua gave to Yochanan.

To the Angel of the Messianic Community in Smyrna

Smyrna is today called the city of Izmir, and it lies about 35 miles north of Ephesus on the Aegean coast of Turkey. It has an excellent harbor. It had a strong allegiance to Rome and in 195 BCE and became the first city in the ancient world to build a temple in honor of Dea

59. Rev 2:6

60. Rev 2:14–15 According to Irenaeus, the Nicolaitans are a heretical gnostic sect founded by one called Nicolas. The Nicolaitans lived lives of unrestrained indulgence teaching that it was permissible to practice adultery and eat things sacrificed to idols.

61. Rev 2:7

Roma. Later in 23 BCE, Smyrna won permission to build a temple to the emperor Tiberius Claudius Nero.

The most famous disciple martyred was Yochanan's own disciple whom he ordained as Bishop of Smyrna: the elderly Polycarp. This faithful martyr was placed upon a pyre to be burned upon his refusal to acknowledge the Caesar of Rome as Lord.

> Here is the message from the First and the Last, who died and came alive again:[62]

We have here an obvious identifying introduction. We know who the First and the Last is, and the congregations are familiar with who it is that died and came alive again. Why did the Master use such an introduction?

> I know how you are suffering and how poor you are (though in fact you are rich!). [63]

As was the Master, who did not have a home of his own,[64] the Smyrna congregation was poor. The Master then tries to remind them that in spite of their economic struggles, they had attained spiritual financial solvency. Ya'akov, the Master's brother, taught these things to the congregations of Israel. He is known to have said:

> Listen, my dear brothers, hasn't God chosen the poor of the world to be rich in faith and to receive the Kingdom which he promised to those who love him?

Yochanan's message continues in verses nine and ten:

> And I know the insults of those who call themselves Jews but aren't - on the contrary, they are a synagogue of the Adversary. Don't be afraid of what you are about to suffer.[65]

62. Rev 2:8
63. Rev 2:9
64. Mt 8:20
65. Rev 2:10

Replacement Theology was already being taught in Yochanan's day. Indeed, many Gentile believers from what today are the countries of Syria, Turkey, Greece, and even later Rome, already felt themselves to be the true seed of the Messianic movement, the true Church that replaced unfaithful Israel. These, at times, even worked in competition with, if not directly against, the Israeli disciples who had left Israel. As these Jewish disciples left behind persecution in the Land in order to follow Yeshua's command to teach Torah to all, they now found themselves at odds for their beliefs, with their brothers from the nations. The Gentile believers felt that their Jewish brothers were too Jewish for their taste. They also believed in a perversion of Paul's letters, which they twisted to teach that that they did not have to be about their food anymore, or have to observe Levitical festivals, or pay attention to many other aspects of Judaism as it was practiced then.[66]

As it is with all the Laws of the Torah, not all laws apply to everyone. Some apply to men, some to women, while others to priests or high priests, some to soldiers, some to judges, some to Israelites, and some to non-Israelites. Where it might be true that some elements of Jewish observance do not apply to the Gentile disciples, because these Israeli apostles fervently continued in their Jewish rituals, practices, and traditions, the non-Jewish believers defined the obedience of their Jewish brothers as "legalism." These non-Jewish disciples, who thought that they replaced Israel, are the ones who the Master refers to as, "those who call themselves Jews but aren't." They were truly not Jewish, but in their arrogance and ignorance, not only did they call themselves Jews, but they harassed, persecuted, and even at times demonized the Jewish disciples. This movement within the disciples could be defined as the birth of Christian Anti-Semitism, a movement Yochanan was very aware of. The Master could certainly relate to the Smyrna congregation in these things.

66. 2 Peter 3:15-16

> Don't be afraid of what you are about to suffer. Look, the Adversary is going to have some of you thrown in prison, in order to put you to the test; and you will face an ordeal for ten days.[67]

Again, the Master encourages the congregations by letting them know what is going to happen to them. Why does this bring them consolation? Whenever something bad happens to us, we wonder if we did something wrong or if HaShem is punishing us. The fact that the Master tells the congregation about the coming trials helps them realize that their trials and tribulations are only because of their adherence to the true worship of ADONAI. It reinforces Paul's message:

> None of you would let these persecutions unsettle him. For you yourselves know that these are bound to come to us.[68]

The message to the Smyrna congregation ends with:

> Remain faithful, even to the point of death; and I will give you life as your crown. Those who have ears, let them hear what the Spirit is saying to the Messianic communities. He who wins the victory will not be hurt at all by the second death.[69]

Again, we must realize that Yeshua is talking to congregation members; to people who have already acknowledged him as Messiah; people who are learning Torah. Yet he tells them that their receiving a crown of life is dependent on them being faithful unto death. He again uses that expression, "he who wins the victory," as a condition to escape the second death, the death that will happen at the end of the thousand-year reign of Messiah on earth. Again, we find the unanswered question, "What does 'win the victory' look like?" We may be able to answer this question as we read through the whole prophecy.

---

67. Rev 2:10
68. 1Thes 3:3
69. Rev 2:10–11

To the Angel of the Messianic Community in Pergamum

Pergamum was a religious center. Both pagan religion and Caesar worship thrived in it. The serpent god of healing, Asclepius, was worshipped there, thus the allusion to the "Adversary's throne."

> Here is the message from the one who has the sharp double-edged sword[70]

The Master introduces himself in an authoritative style. The sharp double-edged sword, "is sharper than any double-edged sword - it cuts right through to where soul meets spirit and joints meet marrow, and it is quick to judge the inner reflections and attitudes of the heart."[71] It's like the officer of the law coming with the weapon of judgment in hand. Yeshua decidedly needs to straighten something out with that congregation.

> I know where you are living, there where the Adversary's throne is. Yet you are holding onto my name. You did not deny trusting me even at the time when my faithful witness Antipas was put to death in your town, there where the Adversary lives.[72]

Not much is known about Antipas. A work called, "The Acts of Antipas" puts him as Bishop of Pergamum. In any case, he was martyred by the Romans for his adherence to the commandment to serve only One God, the God Yeshua taught us to pray to, saying, "Our Father in Heaven." Yeshua commends the congregation for not being shaken due to Antipas' martyrdom.

> Nevertheless, I have a few things against you: you have some people who hold to the teaching of Bil`am, who taught Balak to set a trap for the people of Isra'el, so that they would eat food that had been sacrificed to idols and commit sexual sin.[73]

---

70. Rev 2:12
71. Heb 4:12
72. Rev 2:13
73. Rev 2:14

The congregation was doing well as far as keeping their faith, but it had some theological practices that displeased the Master. Bil'am was a prophet who agreed to prophesy for gain. This may sound wrong, but even today there are self-appointed prophets, who preach for financial gain. The Master uses the story of Bil'am to warn against this practice. Kefa, his disciple, did also.[74]

In the story, Bila'am was paid a very large sum of money by King Balak to curse Israel. Knowing better, at first Bila'am refused, but tempted by his greed, he ended up going anyway. The Bible tells us that every time he got ready to curse the Israelites, HaShem took over his mouth and blessed them instead. Jewish texts tell us that in frustration for not getting his money, Bila'am told Balak that no one could curse those who carry HaShem's name and blessing; that they could only curse themselves through disobedience. Bila'am then suggested that Balak send beautiful women to invite the men of Isra'el to a party in the city. Lured by their sexual lust, the men went after the women and participated in orgies to Ba'al Pe'or, which displeased HaShem. It seems that the Pergamum congregation had teachers who, giving in to financial pressures, either compromised by allowing the practice of deviant sexual practice, or even taught them. The practices in question were:

1. Eat food that had been sacrificed to idols
   - There were two ways one ate food offered to idols. One way was to participate in idol-worship which was forbidden; the other was to buy in the market meat dedicated to an idol.
   - Yeshua expected his congregations to continue in both Torah obligations and rabbinic applications concerning the consumption of food, especially meat.
2. Commit sexual sin.
   - Sexual sin is defined in the Torah as anything other than a hetero-sexual relationship within marriage.

74. Num 22; 25:3; 31:16, 2 Peter 2:15

Paul taught the Roman and the Corinthian congregations along these same lines regarding food and sexual behavior. We see here that these Messianic congregations were expected to be Torah obedient, with sin defined as the breaking of the commandment of Torah.[75] It makes sense, since Yeshua said:

> Don't think that I have come to abolish the Torah or the Prophets. I have come not to abolish but to complete. Yes indeed! I tell you that until heaven and earth pass away, not so much as a yud or a stroke will pass from the Torah — not until everything that must happen has happened.[76]

The oracle continues in verses sixteen and seventeen:

> Therefore, turn from these sins. Otherwise, I will come to you very soon and make war against them with the sword of my mouth. Those who have ears, let them hear what the Spirit is saying to the Messianic communities. To him winning the victory I will give some of the hidden manna. I will also give him a white stone, on which is written a new name that nobody knows except the one receiving it.[77]

The idea here is to turn, to make what is called in Hebrew, *teshuvah* תשובה or, "repentance," which means to turn away from our own works, doctrines, and ways, to serve HaShem according to his commands and demands. If we don't, he certainly makes war with us.[78] And again, the to him winning the victory is the challenge to these Messianic congregations. This time, they who win the victory, get to eat of the "hidden manna."

Yochanan knew where this hidden manna came from. He remembered his childhood days in Torah school with his friends in Galilee. His teacher told him of Moshe who built the Ark of the Covenant, and how he was told to hide a measure of manna in it. Since then, Jewish sages have taught that this manna is reserved

75. 1 John 3:4
76. Mt 5:17–18
77. Rev 2:16–17
78. Lev 26:23–36

for the future, for the World the Come, for the reign of Messiah on earth. Today he is told that Yeshua will only give it to those who win the victory.

With the white stone, Yochanan is reminded of the famous story of King David who took an unauthorized census. The Torah forbids rulers to conduct censuses of HaShem's people. King David was severely punished for it. So, whenever they needed a census, instead of counting people, they counted stones that represented each person. These stones represent us. They are inscribed with our name. It means that if we win the victory, we are part of the population of the Kingdom of Heaven on earth. It refers to the tenth and last census of Israel Jeremiah talks about in the *Acharet-hayamim* אחרת הימים the latter days, the tenth and last census:

> In the cities of the hill-country, in the cities of the Sh'felah, in the cities of the Negev, in the territory of Binyamin, in the areas around Yerushalayim and in the cities of Y'hudah flocks will again pass under the hands of the one who counts them," says ADONAI.[79]

Again, what does "win the victory" look like?

To the Angel of the Messianic Community in Thyatira

The congregation in Thyatira was in a city which was a center where people worshiped the Greek god Apollo. Apollo was known as the son of god. He was supposed to be the son of Zeus. Thyatira was a center for the manufacturing of the image of the all-seeing eye, thus the reference to the "eyes like a fiery flame" in the message given to Yochanan. These are little glass images which are still on sale today for tourists. Thyatira's guild was the manufacturer of purple dye and cloth. Lydia was a dealer in purple cloth from the city of Thyatira.[80] Purple cloth was only worn by the wealthy.[81]

---

79. Jer 33:13
80. Acts 16:14
81. Lu 16:19, Rev 17:4

> Here is the message from the Son of God, whose eyes are like a fiery flame and whose feet are like burnished brass: I know what you are doing, your love, trust, service and perseverance. And I know that you are doing more now than before.[82]

Commendation before rebuke?

> But I have this against you: you continue to tolerate that Izevel woman, the one who claims to be a prophet, but is teaching and deceiving my servants to commit sexual sin and eat food that has been sacrificed to idols. I gave her time to turn from her sin, but she doesn't want to repent of her immorality. So, I am throwing her into a sickbed; and those who commit adultery with her I am throwing into great trouble, unless they turn from the sins connected with what she does; and I will strike her children dead.[83]

Pergamos had people who followed the example of Bila'am. Thyatira had people who followed after that of "Izevel," or Jezebel. Since the letters were written to the leaders of the congregations which were males, commentators have suggested that this Izevel was actually the wife of the leader of the Thyatira congregation. Being indiscriminate about food was already an issue within many of the non-Jewish Messianic congregations. In addition, this congregation of Thyatira seemed to have a problem with sexual sins and immorality. How could this be?

Whether this woman is referred to as Izevel or Jezebel, it may not be her real name. In the true spirit of the adage, a picture is worth a thousand words, the texts from the disciples followed the model of the Jewish prophets who, because of the non-corporeal nature of God, made extensive use of imagery in order to bring their point across. As such, the records of Yeshua's life given us by Yochanan are rich with imagery.

In Yochanan's words, Yeshua refers to himself as a light, a door, or a shepherd, to explain his role in our lives. Yochanan the Immerser,

---

82. Rev 2:18–19
83. Rev 2:20–23

as well as Kefa, referred to the Master as a "spotless lamb going to the slaughter," thus invoking the imagery of the daily tamid offerings in the Temple. Of course, we know that Yeshua is not a light, a door, a shepherd, nor a lamb. He is a human being whose role is explained to us through this imagery. Human sacrifices are abhorrent to HaShem, so Yeshua could not have been literally offered on the Temple altar, but these analogies explain to us how and why he died. Also, human meat is not kosher, so of course he couldn't literally ask us to eat his body or drink his blood;[84] this would be cannibalism. But the Jews who heard these words, including Yochanan who was there that day, understood that he was referring to the role of the peace offering, the only offering that everyone eats.

The name Izevel, gives us many clues as to what was going on in the Pergamum congregation. This is an allusion to the history of Ahab and Izevel as given in 2 Kings 9:1; 10:36. Although we do not know who this Izevel was, from the allusion we may assume that she was a woman of power and influence in Thyatira; a woman who corrupted the true religion, and harassed the followers of Yeshua in that city, just as Izevel did in the Northern Kingdom. In Israel's history, she was the Phoenician wife of Ahab, the king/leader of Israel whom he married for political and trade advantages. The religion she practiced and brought to Israel included the evil worship of the goddess Astarte, or in Hebrew, Ashera/Ashterot, also called in the Bible, the Queen of Heaven. This goddess was an early Semitic representation of its future Asia Minor representations of Diana, Venus, and Aphrodite.

> Then all the Messianic communities will know that I am the one who searches minds and hearts, and that I will give to each of you what your deeds deserve.[85]

It is when judgment comes that we truly know HaShem!

84. Jn 6:54–56
85. Rev 2:23

> But to the rest of you in Thyatira, to those who do not hold this teaching, who have not learned what some people call the deep things of the Adversary, I say this: I am not loading you up with another burden; only hold fast to what you have until I come.[86]

Yochanan often had to face these false apostles teaching the disciples so-called deep things that made them feel more intelligent and knowledgeable than others. He knows how these deep things appeal to our pride, but usually take us away from the simplicity of the Torah, from the simple obedience to the commandments. Sometimes, they even tell us that we don't have to obey the commandments so literally. Yochanan learned as a young child in Torah school that these deep things were the downfall of King Shlomo. He remembered the famous story he was taught about the time when King Shlomo, in obedience to the Torah commandment for every king of Israel to write a copy of the Torah for themselves, had an issue when he came to the verse, "He (the King of Israel) shall not multiply wives." Shlomo, who had countless wives and concubines, felt uncomfortable. As he kept reading, he saw the reason why this commandment was given. It says, "Likewise, he is not to acquire many wives for himself, so that his heart will not turn away."[87] The king thought to himself, "The goal of the commandment is not to forbid me to have many wives, but it is to protect my heart from turning away from God. So, because I am so wise, I will keep my wives, but I will not let my heart turn away. In this manner, the heart of the commandment will be kept."

Yochanan remembers how that went! Shlomo was proud of being so smart as to feel he could circumvent the literal application of the commandment, but because he understood its heart, conviction got the better of him. The literal meaning of the text he was about to write still stared him in the face. This is where he noticed something in the Hebrew, which reads this way: ולא ירבה נשים. He actually noticed that the word "multiply" starts with a yod, and that if you take that yod off, the text reads, "The king has not multiplied wives... ולא רבה נשי."

86. Rev 2:24–25

87. Deut 17:17

Shlomo, then decided to make a little edition to the Torah and erase that bothersome yod. The story goes that this yod was horrified at Shlomo's impertinence.

Yochanan remembers how the Rabbi who taught him that story gesticulated, in all sorts of ways, to express the yod's disgust at such arrogance. The yod went to deposit a formal complaint to the throne that is higher than Shlomo's, the throne of the Almighty. The yod complained, "Why, who does he think he is, King Shlomo or what? I may be the smallest letter of the alphabet and my place in the Torah may even be insignificant, but no one can be allowed to …" The Almighty was listening and urged the yod to calm down with these famous words, "Don't worry little yod! Kings like Shlomo will come and go, but until heaven and earth pass away, not one little yod nor even a tittle of my Torah will pass away."

Now Yochanan remembered his Master using the very same words to tell us that the Torah will remain valid as long as heaven and earth remain functional. By now, Yochanan can almost guess how the message to the congregation will end,

> To him who wins the victory and does what I want until the goal is reached, I will give him authority over the nations; he will rule them with a staff of iron and dash them to pieces like pottery, just as I have received authority from my Father. I will also give him the morning star. Those who have ears, let them hear what the Spirit is saying to the Messianic communities.[88]

If we "win the victory" in Pergamum, we receive a white stone. If we "win the victory" in Thyatira, we receive the Morning Star. Literally, this morning star refers to Venus, the brightest object in the sky after the sun and the moon. It is also the first star to shine at dusk and the last one to disappear after dawn. Later in the text, Yochanan refers to it as the Messiah himself,[89] whose coming was foretold by Bil'am: A star shall step forth out of Jacob.[90] Kefa also referred to it.[91]

88. Rev 2:26–29
89. Rev 22:16
90. Num 24:17
91. 2 Peter 1:19

To the Angel of the Messianic Community in Sardis

Sardis was a fortress built on the top of a high cliff on the slope of Mount Tmolus, about 50 miles east of Smyrna and 30 miles southeast of Thyatira. Sardis had many mystery cults and secret religious societies. It was home to the magnificent Temple of Artemis. Its people were idolaters and worshipped the mother goddess, Cybele, which included orgies during festivals held in her honor. Sardis fell through a false sense of security. Twice in its history, the Acropolis fell to the enemy due to lack of vigilance of its defenders.

Even Cyrus, the king of Persia, was unable to take the city, though he besieged it. The frustrated emperor then threw out the challenge that, "If any man will find a way to storm that fortress and overwhelm it, I will give to him large rewards." One day, one of Cyrus' soldiers on guard duty noticed that one of the Lydian soldiers on top of the cliff dropped his helmet over the battlement as he fell asleep. The helmet fell all the way down to the base of the cliff. The Lydian soldier climbed down to recover his helmet, then climbed back up to his place of sentinel duty. Later that night, the observant Persian guard who had seen the Lydian climb down and back up the cliff took a selected band of soldiers and they made their way up the cliff to the battlement. They found it unguarded, so Sardis fell into the hands of the Persians.

> Here is the message from the one who has the sevenfold Spirit of God and the seven stars… [92]

Again, Yeshua identifies himself to Yochanan. With these words, he establishes that not only is he in control of the archangelic authorities in the heavens, but also of those shepherds leading the congregations on earth. As we see in the next utterances, the Master has a very important warning for the believers in Sardis:

> I know what you are doing - you have a reputation for being alive, but in fact you are dead![93]

92. Rev 3:1
93. Rev 3:1

Yochanan had to deliver these pretty strong words from Yeshua to a congregation with the semblance and reputation of life and godliness, but who, in HaShem's eyes, is dead. How does that happen? Yochanan often saw his Master correct some of their Pharisee brothers who, like the people of Sardis thought of themselves to be doing fine, but whom he defined as blind.[94] As a shepherd to the congregations, Yochanan is well acquainted with human nature, which tends to make us look at ourselves with rose-colored glasses; we easily rationalize our lives and actions to absolve ourselves from the awful realization of our daily failures. But HaShem's Spirit which, cuts right through to where soul meets spirit and joints meet marrow and is quick to judge the inner reflections and attitudes of the heart,[95] doesn't see as man sees. In fact, he tells us that:

> My thoughts are not your thoughts, and your ways are not my ways... As high as the sky is above the earth are my ways higher than your ways, and my thoughts than your thoughts.[96]

The Master also comments:

> You people make yourselves look righteous to others, but God knows your hearts; what people regard highly is an abomination before God![97]

As human beings, we often fall into the fallacy of being right in our own eyes. That is why HaShem decidedly said, "It isn't good that the [man] should be alone. I will make for him a companion suitable for helping him."[98] The Hebrew in this text is even more revealing. It says, לא טוב היות האדם לבד אעשה לו עזר כנגדו. This literally translates, "It is not good for the man to be by himself; I will create him a help to challenge him." That "help" is, in fact, meant to be an element of

94. Mt 25
95. Heb 4:12
96. Isa 55:8–9
97. Lk 16:15
98. Gen 2:18

opposition in order to keep men properly balanced. It works the other way around also!

As a congregation, Sardis may have failed to see itself through the eyes of others and was feeling content and satisfied with its performance. These words from the Master through Yochanan, whom they probably knew and respected, must have been a wake-up call! In fact, the next sentence says:

> Wake up, and strengthen what remains, before it dies too! For I have found what you are doing incomplete in the sight of my God.[99]

This reminds us of the message Paul wrote to the Roman congregation:

> Besides all this, you know at what point of history we stand; so, it is high time for you to rouse yourselves from sleep; for the final deliverance is nearer than when we first came to trust.[100]

As a faithful shepherd concerned for his flock, Yeshua sends a "wakeup" message to the Sardis brethren. He tells them to "wake-up" to their Torah obligations and not be in unconcerned slumber towards them. Yochanan knew the situation. Many of the Jewish disciples who continued teaching a simple, literal obedience to Torah, were slowly but surely belittled by their Gentile brothers. In this warning, the Master tells the Sardis congregation that because they had stopped following Torah, they are asleep. Many of the other good works they did, which made them look good to themselves, were truly good. However, those good works did not replace their obligations towards Torah observance. While they practiced good deeds, they criticized the Jewish disciples who taught them to follow Torah. Now the Master was settling the question. He told them in verse three:

> So remember what you received and heard, and obey it, and turn from your sin! For if you don't wake up, I will come like a thief; and you don't know at what moment I will come upon you.[101]

---

99. Rev 3:2

100. Rom 13:11

101. Rev 3:3

In this passage, Yeshua uses the words, "as a thief," to remind them twice that Sardis' enemies conquered her by surprise because of a slumbering soldier. In this Fall festival season, Yochanan remembers how he celebrated the feasts in his village of Galilee. He reminisces that Rosh Hashanah was difficult to plan, for it came unexpectedly, as a thief in the night. with the birth of the Tishri new moon. His brother in service, Paul, referred to it in a letter to the Thessalonian disciples, ."".. because you yourselves well know that the Day of the Lord will come like a thief in the night."[102] Oh, how important it is to be and stay awake!

Not all of Sardis' disciples were asleep though. The Master continues his message in verse four:

> Nevertheless, you do have a few people in Sardis who have not soiled their clothes; and they will walk with me, clothed in white, because they are worthy.[103]

White linen belonged to priests. Thus, the Master tells these disciples of Sardis, who are faithful to the things they have been taught about Torah, that they will take part in the promise made to Moses: "and you will be a Kingdom of cohanim for me, a nation set apart," which Shim'on Kefa also applied to the faithful disciples of Rome: "But you are a chosen people, the King's cohanim, a holy nation, a people for God to possess."[104]

The Master signs off in verse five with:

> He who wins the victory will, like them, be dressed in white clothing.[105]

The allusion to "white clothing" seems to be the custom by the Jewish Sanhedrin in judging priests fit for service. They examined the priests concerning their genealogies and blemishes. Every priest in whom was found anything faulty in his genealogy was clothed in black and

---

102. 1 Thes 5:2
103. Rev 3:4
104. Exod 19:6; 1 Peter 2:9
105. Rev 3:5

veiled in black, and was put out of the court, but everyone that was found perfect and right: he was clothed in white ילבש בגדים לבנים. Let us remember again that disciples of the Master are destined to become priests. This white clothing represents also the righteous deeds of God's people.[106]Isaiah speaks of this white linen:

> I am so joyful in ADONAI! My soul rejoices in my God, for he has clothed me in salvation, dressed me with a robe of triumph, like a bridegroom wearing a festive turban, like a bride adorned with her jewels.[107]

The priestly white linen garment comes in contrast with the defiled garment that Jude, the Master's brother, speaks to us about: "hating even the clothes stained by their vices."[108] Our garment is stained when we live by the vices of the world instead of by the virtues of the Torah.

> And I will not blot his name out of the Book of Life; in fact, I will acknowledge him individually before my Father and before his angels. Those who have ears, let them hear what the Spirit is saying to the Messianic communities.[109]

Much was at stake indeed. Yochanan understood the seriousness of the message. Unless the brethren "win the victory," they partake neither of the priesthood nor of the promises of rewards for good deeds. Their names are blotted out of the Book of Life. Yeshua does not acknowledge them before the father.

This made for a very special Rosh Hashanah season for Yochanan. He knew that the months of Elul and Tishrei are the times when we enter judgment with HaShem. At the end of the season, our names are written either in the Book of Life, in the Book of Death, or in the Book of "In-Betweens." He remembers how Daniel the prophet makes reference to these books: Then the court was convened, and the books were opened.[110] Yochanan is also aware that not only our

106. Rev 19:8
107. Isaiah 61:10
108. Judg 23
109. Rev 3:5–6
110. Dan 7:10

name can be blotted from one book and written into another but that the presence of our name in the Book of Life depends on the Master's acknowledgment of us to the Father.

What does this mean then if we don't "win the victory"? Does it mean he will not acknowledge us individually before his Father or before his angels? What does "win the victory" look like?

To the Angel of the Messianic Community in Philadelphia

Philadelphia is modern day Alaþehir. Its name is derived from Attalus II (159-138 B.C.E.), whose truth and loyalty to his brother, Eumenes, won him the epithet Philadelphus which means, brotherly love. Being on a major trade route it was an ideal place for the spreading of new ideas and creeds.

> Here is the message of HaKadosh, the True One, the one who has the key of David.[111]

Yochanan often used the term HaKadosh Baruch Hu, the "Blessed and Holy-One" while praying. Here Yeshua says to him, "Here says HaShem, the Holy One...," thus stressing to the apostle that he is telling a message he received from the Father. Yochanan also remembers Isaiah's use of the term *Kadosh Israel* קדוש ישראל when prophesying about Messiah. Having studied Isaiah's prophecies, Yochanan understands the reference to "the Key of David." He can still hear his Torah teacher expounding on Isaiah 22 where Shebna, the treasurer of the Household of David, has been removed and his post given to Eliakim. Eliakim then became the custodian of the Key of David, which gave him all authority over the goods of the House of David. Yochanan knows that HaShem certainly is the One who owns the Key of David's household or dynasty, the One who brings to fruition the Davidic Messianic promises, the One

> ...who, if he opens something, no one else can shut it, and if he closes something, no one else can open it.[112]

111. Rev 3:7
112. Rev 3:7

Yeshua continued delivering the Father's message in verse eight.

> I know what you are doing. Look, I have put in front of you an open door, and no one can shut it.[113]

Yochanan is glad to acknowledge and even confirm the congregation's efforts. Their geographic location on a major trade route was ideal; a true open door to reach many diaspora Jews and non-Jews of the area with the teachings of the Master. They were receiving much persecution, which caused them to remain poor and weak, but they were staying faithful:

> I know that you have but little power, yet you have obeyed my message and have not disowned me. Here, I will give you some from the synagogue of the Adversary, those who call themselves Jews but aren't — on the contrary, they are lying - see, I will cause them to come and prostrate themselves at your feet, and they will know that I have loved you.[114]

Yochanan was also aware that in this congregation, as in others, there was a problem with Gentile believers claiming to have replaced Israel for the favors of HaShem and therefore, persecuting their Jewish brothers and sisters. Yochanan knew the story too well. It was nothing new. It was the story of jealousy against the chosen firstborn which goes back to Ishma'el being jealous of Isaac; Esau of Jacob; and of Joseph's brothers who were jealous of his firstborn status. "How long will this narrative continue?" he must have thought! "It has already gone on for nearly 2,000 years!"

Looking at the faithful Philadelphians doing their best in spite of their condition, Yochanan must have bemoaned the jealousy of human nature that always wants what it does not have. Already in Philadelphia, the Western non-Jewish believers chafed at the Jews for their firstborn status. These apostates went as far as actually claiming to be Jewish; but Yeshua says that they are not! Yochanan was present in Jerusalem on that day not long after the resurrection of the Master, when Paul

113. Rev 3:8
114. Rev 3:8–9

presented Titus to the leaders Kefa, Yochanan, and Ya'akov, in order to showcase the faithful non-Jewish disciples from Galatia.

Paul was greeted with resistance when he pleaded for the insertion of the Greek disciples in the national life of Israel.[115] Ya'akov stood up for them, and with a few food related requirements to their already acquired Noahide halacha, these non-Jewish disciples were received and accepted by the Jewish disciples.[116] But now in Philadelphia, the non-Jewish disciples not only rejected their Jewish brothers, but claimed to replace them in the sight of God. Because of their arrogance and resistance to the will of God, HaShem nicknamed them the "Synagogue (assembly) of the Adversary" (in Hebrew: HaSatan). Yochanan is glad to deliver a message of encouragement to the Philadelphian brothers. In this oracle, HaShem encourages the Philadelphians. He tells them that these apostates will eventually prostrate to them, acknowledging that HaShem loves Israel and has not rejected his people![117]

> Because you did obey my message about persevering, I will keep you from the time of trial coming upon the whole world to put the people living on earth to the test.[118]

This phrase uses a play on words with Hebrew:

יען שמרת דבר סבלנותי אשמרך גם־אני משעת הנסיון העתידה
לבוא על־תבל כלה לנסות את־ישבי הארץ

The literal text reads, "Because you have kept the word of my patience, I will also keep you from the tribulation that will come upon the whole world." This must have been such an encouragement for the Philadelphian brothers and sisters. Yochanan saw them patiently "take it on the chin," in the way that Yeshua and Paul had taught. They did not return evil for evil but overcame evil with good. They did not curse their enemies but prayed for them. They did not

115. Eph 2:11-14
116. Acts 15
117. Rom 11:1
118. Rev 3:10

allow themselves to hate their enemies, and at times may even have helped them. Struck on one cheek, they turned the other; asked to carry a load one mile, they carried it two. It is at such a time that our obedience to the words of the Master is tested. The Philadelphians did not give in to the evils of revenge-seeking, of bitterness, and of hatred. They followed the examples of Abraham who allowed himself to be cheated by the Canaanites when he agreed to pay an exorbitant price for a piece of land to bury his wife, when by divine right, that land was his. The Philadelphians went after the ways of Isaac, who did not seek to avenge himself from those who stole his wells, but actually set a meal before them. They followed Jacob, who humbled himself before Esau; after Joseph who did not punish his brothers. As such, they were perfect. They accomplished and kept the words and the patience of the Master:

> You have heard that our fathers were told, Eye for eye and tooth for tooth. But I tell you not to stand up against someone who does you wrong. On the contrary, if someone hits you on the right cheek, let him hit you on the left cheek too! If someone wants to sue you for your shirt, let him have your coat as well! And if a soldier forces you to carry his pack for one mile, carry it for two! When someone asks you for something, give it to him; when someone wants to borrow something from you, lend it to him. You have heard that our fathers were told, Love your neighbor - and hate your enemy. But I tell you, love your enemies! Pray for those who persecute you! Then you will become children of your Father in heaven. For he makes his sun shine on good and bad people alike, and he sends rain to the righteous and the unrighteous alike. What reward do you get if you love only those who love you? Why, even tax-collectors do that! And if you are friendly only to your friends, are you doing anything out of the ordinary? Even the Goyim do that! Therefore, be perfect, just as your Father in heaven is perfect.[119]

119. Mt 5:38–48

They were persecuted wrongly by their own brethren, as well as by the government, but they believed in the words from Shim'on Kefa:

> For it is a grace when someone, because he is mindful of God, bears up under the pain of undeserved punishment. For what credit is there in bearing up under a beating you deserve for doing something wrong? But if you bear up under punishment, even though you have done what is right, God looks on it with favor. Indeed, this is what you were called to; because the Messiah too suffered, on your behalf, leaving an example so that you should follow in his steps. "He committed no sin, nor was any deceit found on his lips." When he was insulted, he didn't retaliate with insults; when he suffered, he didn't threaten, but handed them over to him who judges justly.[120]

This attitude proves their deep trust in HaShem. Yeshua then encourages them by telling them of his own return:

> I am coming soon; hold on to what you have, so that no one will take away your crown.[121]

And again, Yeshua utters the same challenge:

> I will make him who wins the victory a pillar in the Temple of my God, and he will never leave it.[122]

Yeshua encourages the Philadelphians with the promise that if they "win the victory," they will become an ornamental pillar in HaShem's Temple, thus contributing to its strength and beauty.

> Also, I will write on him the name of my God and the name of my God's city, the new Yerushalayim coming down out of heaven from my God, and my own new name.[123]

120. 1 Pet 2:19–23
121. Rev 3:11
122. Rev 3:12
123. Rev 3:12

The victorious will be branded with HaShem's glorious name. They become his property and citizens of his city, Jerusalem, the city that Abraham the faithful looked for, and even saw in a vision.

> By trusting, Avraham obeyed, after being called to go out to a place which God would give him as a possession; indeed, he went out without knowing where he was going. By trusting, he lived as a temporary resident in the Land of the promise, as if it were not his, staying in tents with Yitz'chak and Ya`akov, who were to receive what was promised along with him. For he was looking forward to the city with permanent foundations, of which the architect and builder is God. [124]
>
> Those who have ears, let them hear what the Spirit is saying to the Messianic communities.[125]

To the Angel of the Messianic Community in Laodicea

Unlike the other congregations, Laodicea never personally met Paul.[126] They were supposed to read the letter that the apostle sent to the Colossians, and the Colossians were supposed to read the letter sent to the Laodicean congregation. We still have the letter to the Colossians, but so far, the one sent to Laodicea has not been found.[127]

The city had an extensive business in the production of wool cloth. When it was destroyed by an earthquake in C.E. 60 it was able to rebuild itself without outside help.

> Here is the message from the Amen, the faithful and true witness, the Ruler of God's creation.[128]

To Laodicea, Yeshua introduces himself as the "Amen," in other words, the "One in whom you can believe and trust; he who has the true teaching" and is the "True Witness," the "Ruler of God's creation."

---

124. Heb 11:8–10
125. Rev 3:13
126. Col 2:1
127. Col 4:16
128. Rev 3:14

This was a very authoritative introduction. Yochanan remembers the times when the Master used such strong language. It was when he had a rather strong message to deliver. This "Amen" is the true witness who tells HaShem about us, and he rules over HaShem's creation. Yochanan reminisces over the seven things he learned that HaShem created even before he set to work on the heavens and the earth. The first of these seven was the name of Messiah. Yochanan, a faithful Talmud student, knew about this. In his narrative of the life of the Master he writes:

> In the beginning was the Word, and the Word was with God, and the Word was God. He was with God in the beginning. All things came to be through him, and without him nothing made had being.[129]

Yochanan made wise use of the word Memra (Word) that the sages who wrote the Aramaic Targum introduced to represent any physical representation of HaShem in the Tanakh so they wouldn't need to use his Name. From Abraham's strange visitors, Moshe's burning bush, to the apparition of a fourth person in Nebuchadnezzar's fiery furnace everybody understood what the Memra was. Any time the Tanakh spoke of HaShem in physical terms, the sages used the Aramaic expression, "the Memra." In the Targum, the Memra figures constantly as the manifestation of the divine power, or as HaShem's messenger in his place. So, when Yochanan tried to explain Messiah to his Jewish brethren, he spoke of the "Memra/the Word." Through this connection, Jews who were familiar with the Memra understood the role and place of Messiah in the Tanakh, and in their lives. Later, Yochanan also mentions:

> Everyone living on earth will worship it except those whose names are written in the Book of Life belonging to the Lamb slaughtered before the world was founded.[130]

129. Jn 1:1–3
130. Rev 13:8

The Lamb/Memra/Messiah was slaughtered before the world was founded. Yochanan has no doubt as to the origins of the letters.

> I know what you are doing: you are neither cold nor hot. How I wish you were either one or the other! So, because you are lukewarm, neither cold nor hot, I will vomit you out of my mouth![131]

Yochanan knew that the congregation lived in a region with nearby hot springs, which delivered cool water to the city. Whereas this cool water brought a certain element of comfort to their daily life, the Master describes the congregation as fireless and complacent. The Master tells the congregation that they would be better off as enemies, that he couldn't stand their lukewarmness. The apostle had seen it before: comfort, wealth, and security weaken one's convictions; this is spiritually dangerous when you live in a culture so opposite to yours. Yochanan taught the believers that they were to be a counter-culture society; they needed to be strong, not weak.

> For you keep saying, "I am rich, I have gotten rich, I don't need a thing!" You don't know that you are the one who is wretched, pitiable, poor, blind and naked! My advice to you is to buy from me gold refined by fire, so that you may be rich.[132]

Yochanan lived a very austere life. Like Paul, he refused to live at the charge of the brethren and worked for a living stoking the fires at a Roman bath house. He might have seen what opulence does to character. Living in such a financial banking hub as Laodicea, the brethren felt comfortable. But with financial security come arrogance, pride, selfishness, complacency, and often corruption. In the Laodiceans, who lived by the mercies of the local hot springs, Yochanan may have seen the Egyptians of old who lived at ease, not because of honest hard work, but because of the never-failing yearly overflowing of the Nile. Their advantageous geographic location caused them to become proud. Their self-sufficiency caused them to be arrogant. The divine message given to them tells them to buy gold tried by fire, the tempered

131. Rev 3:15–16
132. Rev 3:17–18

gold of the wealth of Torah deeds.[133] Ya'akov, whom Yochanan knew well, also despised the admiration of worldly wealth. He said:

> Listen, my dear brothers, hasn't God chosen the poor of the world to be rich in faith and to receive the Kingdom which he promised to those who love him? But you despise the poor! Aren't the rich the ones who oppress you and drag you into court?[134]

For both the Master and Ya'akov, physical wealth was equal to spiritual poverty, while physical poverty was equal to spiritual wealth!

> ...and white clothing, so that you may be dressed and not have to be ashamed of your nakedness.[135]

Because of the city's wool cloth production, even clothing was more easily available and maybe even less expensive than in other places. But for the Master, it seems that one who is richly dressed may be spiritually naked (void of the good works of Torah), while he who is actually physically naked (due to poverty) may be the one who is rich in faith. Yochanan remembered the precious words of the Master, "You can't be a slave to both God and money."[136]

> ...and eye salve to rub on your eyes, so that you may see.[137]

Though Laodicea was famous for its eye salve that helped cure bad eyesight, Yeshua considers them blind, spiritually blind. Yochanan again remembers the words of the Master calling "blind" those who were ignorant of the true spirit of the Torah. In the eyes of the Master, though physically rich, dressed, and seeing, Laodicea is poor, naked, and blind!

> As for me, I rebuke and discipline everyone I love; so exert yourselves, and turn from your sins! Here, I'm standing at the door, knocking. If someone hears my voice and opens the door, I will come in to him and eat with him, and he will eat with me.[138]

133. 1 Cor 3:11–15
134. Jas 2:5–6
135. Rev 3:18
136. Mt 6:13
137. Rev 3:18
138. Rev 3:19–20

As a faithful shepherd Yochanan is eager to receive the repenting soul. He knows that as the apostle said, ADONAI disciplines those he loves and whips everyone he accepts as a son,[139] a language that mirrors that of Shlomo the King of Israel, For ADONAI corrects those he loves like a father who delights in his son.[140] This gift of repentance, Yochanan learned, is one of the seven things HaShem made before the creation of the world. As the old apostle hears these words from Yeshua to Laodicea, he remembers the old teachings about this "door":

> God said to the Israelites, My children, open to me one door of repentance, even so wide as the eye of a needle, and I will open to you doors through which calves and horned cattle may pass.[141]
>
> If a man conceal his sin, and does not open it before the holy King, although he ask mercy, yet the door of repentance shall not be opened to him. But if he open it before the holy blessed God, God spares him, and mercy prevails over wrath; and when he laments, although all the doors were shut, yet they shall be opened to him, and his prayer shall be heard.[142]

Ya'akov also spoke in the same terms:

> Don't grumble against one another, brothers, so that you won't come under condemnation — look! The Judge is standing at the door![143]

Laodicea is also challenged in verse twenty-two with:

> I will let him who wins the victory sit with me on my throne, just as I myself also won the victory and sat down with my Father on his throne. Those who have ears, let them hear what the Spirit is saying to the Messianic communities.[144]

Again, what does "win the victory" look like?

139. Heb 12:6
140. Prov 3:12
141. Shir Hashirim Rabba, fol. 25, 1
142. Sohar Levit, fol. 8, col. 32
143. Jas 5:9
144. Rev 3:21–22

Thoughts from the Author

Yeshua's messages to the congregations through Yochanan involve prophetic warnings concerning their immediate tragic future. These messages of preparation contain the issues that they need to address in order to be ready to face this future. Faithful application and adherence to the corrections given in these messages define what it means to "win the victory."

Here is a seven-point summary of what Yeshua says the congregations need to correct:

- Their passion for the Master had cooled off
- They strayed from the simple teaching of literal obedience to the Torah of Moshe and they ate ceremonially unclean meat
- They allowed greed and lust to motivate their lives and theology
- They dabbled in idolatry, immorality, and fornication
- They were complacent in their wealth
- They believed that they replaced Israel
- They persecuted the Jewish disciples of the Master

Only obedience to these corrections will allow the disciples:

- To be given the right to eat of the Tree of Life which is in God's Gan-Eden (Ephesus)
- To not be hurt at all by the second death (Smyrna)
- To eat of the "Hidden Manna," and to obtain citizenship in the Kingdom of God through their name written on a white stone
- To have authority over the nations (Pergamum)
- To fulfill Moshe's prophecy and become priests, not blotted out of the Book of Life (Pergamum)
- To become a "pillar" in HaShem's Temple (Philadelphia)
- To sit on HaShem's throne with Mashiach (Laodicea)

The questions are:

- Could this divine advice also be useful to us today, to us who are closer to the day of the return of Yeshua than those congregations ever were?
- Will we miss these rewards given only to those who "win the victory" if we don't?

Chapter 2
Visiting The Throne Room

- The Throne Room
- The Encampment and the Marching Orders
- The Sealed Book
- The Tzaddik Hador
- A Heavenly Service
- The Fall Feasts

The Throne Room

> And the voice like a trumpet which I had heard speaking with me before said, Come up here. (Rev 4:1)

Now Yochanan is invited to the throne room. He must feel like Moshe whom HaShem invited to "come up."[1] The faithful old disciple probably thinks to himself, "Wow! When Moshe was asked to build the Tabernacle, he was told to do it exactly as was shown him on the Mount.[2] Am I now going to see the original?" There is a midrash that imagines Moshe asking HaShem, "Exactly like you show me? How can I replicate heavenly things using earthly material?" To which HaShem answers, "Like a mirror!" The idea is that in a mirror, we can see things; things even bigger than the mirror itself. What Moshe had built, the Ark, the Tabernacle, the altar, the organization of the whole encampment, was a mirror image of what he had witnessed on the

1. Exod 24:1-2
2. Exod 25:40; 26:30

mount. Yochanan may have also been familiar with Paul's words, For now we see obscurely in a mirror, but then it will be face to face. Now I know partly; then I will know fully, just as God has fully known me.[3]

Yochanan did see the original! As he did, he must have felt like Isaiah, Ezekiel, Daniel, and all the others who were told to "come up" and see the throne room, the place of the Almighty.

> And I will show you what must happen after these things.[4]

Not only was he honored with such a privilege, but Yochanan was now going to get precious intelligence, information he would be able to pass on to the congregations. This information would be crucial to their preparation. It will represent a strong incentive to apply the advice they had just received through the messages.

> Instantly I was in the Spirit, and there before me in heaven stood a throne, and on the throne Someone was sitting. The One sitting there gleamed like diamonds and rubies, and a rainbow shining like emerald encircled the throne. (Rev 4:2–3)

Now it is given to Yochanan to not only hear about, not only to observe, but to experience Isaiah's vision: I saw ADONAI sitting on a high, lofty throne! The hem of his robe filled the temple.[5] At that moment, the ancient prophet saw, above the dome that was over their heads was something like a throne that looked like a sapphire. On it, above it, was what appeared to be a person. I saw what looked like gleaming, amber-colored fire radiating from what appeared to be his waist upward. The vision became so real to him that he had the same reaction as Ezekiel. This was how the appearance of the glory of ADONAI looked. When I saw it, I fell on my face.[6]

The amber-colored fire in the Hebrew description of Ezekiel's vision is described with the word, *ein chashmal* עין חשמל. Chashmal (a biblical Hebrew word which today means "electricity") is used in the Tanakh to speak of heavenly beings. These beings may be given that name because of their possible amber/bronze color. Other such beings

3. 1 Cor 13:12
4. Rev 4:1
5. Isa 6:1
6. Ezek 1:26–28; Rev 1:17

are "seraphim" or "the burning ones," who are related to this amber, golden color of fire. It seems that many things representing HaShem's realm have that color. The golden cloud of the Shekinah comes to mind as well as the oil of anointing, as do the elements of the Temple made of pure gold, and the nightly fire that accompanied the Children of Israel in the desert. That may explain the ancient fascination with gold, and why the "golden" calf was all the more an abomination.

Because we know that Moshe was to build everything according to the model he had seen on the Mount, we can assume that the Tabernacle set-up was, in essence, a pattern of the heavenly reality, a small physical earthly replica. Paul broached that principle when he proclaimed that, ever since the creation of the universe his [HaShem's] invisible qualities — both his eternal power and his divine nature - have been clearly seen, because they can be understood from what he has made. [7]

> Surrounding the throne were twenty-four other thrones, and on the thrones sat twenty-four elders dressed in white clothing and wearing gold crowns on their heads.[8]

The Tabernacle was eventually replaced by the Temple. HaShem gave King David the exact liturgical plan for this temple, which included twenty-four courses of priests, each course being represented by an elder priest. This ensured that every Levitical priest in Israel had a chance to serve at least once a year in the Jerusalem Temple. Yochanan saw the heavenly origin of the earthly priesthood serving while clothed in white linen. They wore gold crowns as a reminder that not only the Levitical priesthood, but also the priesthood of Messiah, is a "royal priesthood."[9]

> From the throne came forth lightnings, voices and thunderings; and before the throne were seven flaming torches, which are the sevenfold Spirit of God.[10]

---

7. Rom 1:20
8. Rev 4:4
9. 1 Chron 25:1 Peter 2:9
10. Rev 4:5

When the children of Israel came to visit HaShem's makeshift camp in the wilderness they were greeted with thunder, lightning and a thick cloud on the mountain. Then a shofar blast sounded so loudly that all the people in the camp trembled.[11]In the seven flaming torches, Yochanan could see the seven-branched candelabrum Moshe was asked to build.[12]

> In front of the throne was what looked like a sea of glass, clear as crystal.[13]

When Moshe and seventy-four elders ate with HaShem on the mountain, they saw the God of Isra'el. Under his feet was something like a sapphire stone pavement as clear as the sky itself.[14]

> In the center, around the throne, were four living beings covered with eyes in front and behind. The first living being was like a lion, the second living being was like an ox, the third living being had a face that looked human, and the fourth living being was like a flying eagle. Each of the four living beings had six wings and was covered with eyes inside and out; and day and night they never stop saying, "Holy, holy, holy is ADONAI, God of heaven's armies the One who was, who is and who is coming!" [15]

The Encampment and the Marching Orders

The encampment of the children of Israel in the desert followed a particular pattern, as seen by Moshe on Mount Horeb, as well as in the four faces of the living beings around the throne. This pattern was like the ancient military encampments with the headquarters well protected in the middle of the camp. The plan was according to the following from the center outward:

11. Exod 19:16
12. Exod 37:17-18
13. Rev 4:6
14. Exod 24 :10
15. Rev 4:6–8

- The Tabernacle
- The Levites surrounded the Tabernacle.
- The tribes surrounded the Levites in a square formation with three tribes on each side of the square.
- Each side was represented by its middle tribe, which was the chief tribe.

Including the tribes of Ephraim and Manasseh, which Jacob adopted as his own children, this makes a total of thirteen tribes. At that time, the children of Israel were also asked to make standards to represent each tribe.[16] These tribal standards were not randomly picked. They matched the blessings given each of them by both Ya'akov and Moshe.[17] Not only did the images on these standards have connection with the faces of the Cherubim around the throne, but they also matched the four sides of what Yo'av calls "the Mazzaroth," the zodiac constellations.[18] When Bila'am saw Israel's encampment in the desert, whose pattern carried the design of HaShem's throne room, he burst into uncontainable praises.[19] Even the heavens declare the beauty and glory of God in Israel's encampment![20] Seeing the heavenly prototypes of the things he knew on earth and in the skies, Yochanan must have literally been in "Heaven"! Truly, we can see why.

> Whenever the living beings give glory, honor and thanks to the One sitting on the throne, to the One who lives forever and ever, the twenty-four elders fall down before the One sitting on the throne, who lives forever and ever, and worship him. They throw their crowns in front of the throne and say, "You are worthy, ADONAI Eloheinu, to have glory, honor and power, because you created all things — yes, because of your will they were created and came into being!"[21]

16. Num 2:2
17. Gen 34; Deut 33
18. Job 38:32
19. Num 24:5
20. Ps 19:1
21. Rev 4:9–11

In the Book of Numbers, Israel is given its marching orders. We must remember that Israel's preparation in the desert was of a military nature; it was that of an army taking over the Land. While the Levites dismantled the tabernacle and carried its furnishings and contents in the heart of the tribes, the tribe of Judah led the way forward. Judah would then lead the way into the Land. Judah would literally lead the charge. Later in our text, our Master shows Yochanan the final fulfillment of all the prophecies given to Abraham and all the prophets. We see this fulfillment as King Yeshua, the Lion of the Tribe of Judah. He leads the charge into the land at the battle of Armageddon. He leads the charge followed by the "host of Heaven," the rest of the tribes. At the very end, following the tribes, comes HaShem's true Tabernacle to dwell among man.[22] Indeed, HaShem doesn't establish his city on earth until the righteousness of Mashiach covers the earth as the waters cover the sea, at a time when there will be no more seas![23]

If Yochanan had doubts before, now he was sure he was seeing the same scene that was shown to Ezekiel.[24] How exhilarated Yochanan must have felt to hear the cherubim saying, Holy, holy, holy is ADONAI, God of heaven's armies, the One who was, who is and who is coming, just like the worship of the priests in the Temple.

The Sealed Book

Yochanan, who was present at the time the Master was transfigured on the mountain,[25] was now made privy to things even the old prophets longed to see. As Moshe was told to "come up," so was Yochanan. As Moshe was allowed to behold the throne room when on the Mount, so was Yochanan. As Moshe received stone tablets containing very important instructions concerning Israel's present and future, so Yochanan would hear very pertinent words to be shared with congregations both present and future.[26]

---

22. Rev 19:11–21, Rev 21:22
23. Rev 21:1
24. Ezek 1:5–11
25. Mt 17:5
26. Rev 1:19

> Next, I saw in the right hand of the One sitting on the throne a scroll with writing on both sides and sealed with seven seals. And I saw a mighty angel proclaiming in a loud voice, "Who is worthy to open the scroll and break its seals?" [27]

A Roman sealed document could only be opened by a person with qualifications equal or superior to the one who sealed it. For example, only a city judge or a superior judge can open a document sealed by a city judge, and only a federal judge or superior can open one sealed by a federal judge. In this case, HaShem is the one who sealed the document and of course, no one holds equal qualifications, as Yochanan sadly discovered:

> No one in heaven, on earth or under the earth was able to open the scroll or look inside it. I cried and cried, because no one was found worthy to open the scroll or look inside it. (Rev. 5:4-3)

Acquiring the information contained in this book was the reason for Yochanan's journey to the throne room. It contained vital information for all the congregations. Yochanan had been promised that enlightenment, but now it was inaccessible due to the lack of qualification. The faithful disciple was so concerned about it that, as it is recorded in verse four, he wept. He knew the information in the book would inspire and motivate the congregations to obey what they had been told in the previous communications.

At that point, Yochanan might have remembered the prophet Daniel, who after receiving a message containing vital information concerning Israel's future was told, But you, Dani'el, keep these words secret, and seal up the book until the time of the end.[28] Yochanan might have wondered, "Is the book in the hand of that is on the Throne the same as Daniel's hidden prophecy book? Is this book destined for this time?

---

27. Rev. 5:1–2
28. Dan 12:4

The Tzaddik Hador

> One of the elders said to me, "Don't cry. Look, the Lion of the tribe of Y'hudah, the Root of David, has won the right to open the scroll and its seven seals." (Rev 5:5)

Yochanan weeps until one of the twenty-four priestly elders addresses him with comforting words, saying that his beloved Master had earned the right and privilege to open the sealed document. His Master was "equal to the task," so to speak. The Master here is inferred by the imagery of the standard of the tribe of Y'hudah. This standard drew its inspiration from the prophetic words of the patriarch Ya'akov: a lion.[29] How did the Master earn the right to open the book? We are told Yeshua earned the right to unseal and open the book through his unmerited suffering. In fact, now more than ever, the old disciple understood the purpose of the cruel unwarranted suffering his Master had endured. In the Jewish mind of the day, suffering was the result of sin,[30] and his Master was unjustly given to endure the suffering deserved by one who is the worst of all criminals. Yochanan was also aware of this old Talmudic teaching that declares that the "suffering of the righteous atones for the sinner":

> Why is the story of Miriam's death placed next to the laws of the red heifer? This is to teach you that just as the red heifer brought atonement, so does the death of the righteous bring atonement. Why is the story of Aaron's death followed by the story of the transfer of his priestly garments? This is to teach you that just as the priest's garments were meant to bring atonement, so too the death of the righteous brings atonement.

During this time of the Fall Festivals, the time nearing Yom Kippur, Yochanan could imagine his Master in the functions of the holy High-Priest of Israel. With nostalgy his mind might have wandered back to Jerusalem, remembering the many Yom Kippurs he spent there. He knew the High-Priest's very important role on that day to offer korbanot for himself, for his household, and finally, and for all

29. Gen 49:9
30. Jn 9:2

of Israel's sins and impurities. Of course, the High-Priest had not committed each and every sin the people of Israel had committed, but he represented them all as one nation. Yochanan then remembered the Yom Kippur prayer when the High Priest identifies with the nation as he says, "I have sinned with all Israel." This is reminiscent to the time when Moshe identified with Israel in the sin of the golden calf, though he had not participated in it. In doing so, he applied the great favor he had received from HaShem onto all Israel, so the nation would not be destroyed.[31] Until this day, the Chassidim teach that:

> In every generation, a tzaddik hador ("the righteous one of the generation") צדיק הדור arises. This is a completely righteous person who becomes the shepherd and leader for a particular generation. The tzaddik hador might be called upon to suffer and die for the sins of his generation: "When there are righteous men in the generation, the righteous are seized by death for the sins of the generation." Likewise, the mystic, Rabbi Moshe Chaim Luzzatto, wrote: "As a result of this principle, suffering and pain may be imposed on a tzaddik (righteous person) as atonement for his entire generation. This tzaddik must then accept this suffering with love for the benefit of his generation, just as he accepts the suffering imposed upon him for his own sake. In doing so, he benefits his generation by atoning for it, and at the same time is himself elevated to a very great degree. For a tzaddik such as this is made into one of the leaders in the Community of the Future World.[32]

Suffering is the mark of the tzaddik. In fact, it is also the mark of the disciples of Yeshua.[33] Suffering, especially suffering unjustly, is a marking of our appurtenance to HaShem. There is an old midrash conjecturing about the time when, just before entering the Land, Moshe hears of Israel's future exile.[34] In the midrash, Moshe asks HaShem:

> Will not the time come when Israel shall have neither Tabernacle nor Temple? What will happen with them then?" The Holy One,

31. Exod 32:33
32. Derech HaShem 2:3
33. 2 Tim 3:12; 1 Peter 2:19–21
34. Deut 32

> blessed be He, replied, "I will then take one of their righteous men and retain him as a pledge on their behalf, in order that I may pardon all their sins."[35]

Yochanan saw his beloved Master as that Tzaddik who has voluntarily suffered for his generation. He is that righteous man retained as a pledge on their behalf, that HaShem may forgive the sins of the nation. He is the tzaddik hador for his generation, who has earned the right and privilege to open the book that will be substantial in saving the people from spiritual annihilation. As he became part of this vision, Yochanan identified his Master by the throne:

> Then I saw standing there with the throne and the four living beings, in the circle of the elders, a Lamb that appeared to have been slaughtered.[36]

Isaiah's words must have resonated in Yochanan's heart: Though mistreated, he was submissive — he did not open his mouth. Like a lamb led to be slaughtered, like a sheep silent before its shearers, he did not open his mouth.[37] This all happened around the festival of Rosh Hashanah, or in Hebrew, Yom Teruah. Ten days after Yom Teruah came the great and awesome day of Yom Kippur. Yochanan perhaps reflected on the ritual of the two goats that Moshe instructed the High-Priest about. One of the goats was to be presented alive to make atonement for the people of Israel.[38]

In the teachings of Derech HaShem, the sages tell the following Yom Kippur midrash where they propose that HaSatan challenges HaShem's sense of justice: "Is this true justice that you destroy the Egyptians because of idolatry when the children of Israel are guilty of the same? HaShem then refutes the accusation by throwing Job at him. Of course, Job and Moshe did not live at the same time, but it is the nature of midrash to not necessarily be chronologically correct. In midrashes, individuals represent ideas or virtues. In this case, Job represents unwarranted suffering. He is one who suffered, although, as

35. Exod Rabbah 35:4
36. Rev. 5:6
37. Isa 53:7
38. Lev 16:8–10

the text says, he was pure and upright.[39] According to Jewish theology, the suffering of the righteous atones for the sinner, therefore if Job was righteous, his suffering could atone for Israel.

In this midrash, the sages use the analogy of a shepherd helping his flock across a river. As he does, a wolf arrives on the scene. The wolf of course preys on the weak, on those who lag. In such a case, the shepherd would offer an old mature goat to the predator, who would be faced with a substantial fight for his dinner. While the predator is kept at bay "negotiating the issue" with the old goat, the shepherd quickly helps the flock across the river. It is afterward, when all the sheep are safely on the other side that he comes to rescue the now beaten and wounded goat. The goat, in a sense, laid down its life for the safety of the rest of the flock. As Yochanan saw the Lamb "save the day," so to speak, through having earned the qualifications to open the book in the hands of the Ancient of Days, these ancient stories must have made much more sense to him.

In school, the disciple had learned about the two Messiahs of Judaism: Mashiach ben Joseph, משיח בן יוסף the Suffering Servant who suffers for the sake of all, and Mashiach ben David the Conquering King משיח בן דוד who brings justice and restoration to all. Yochanan had lived with Mashiach ben Joseph, and now he was given to experience Mashiach ben David. He could see both messianic concepts in the sole person of his Master as described in the experience of which he was made to partake: "Look, the Lion of the tribe of Y'hudah … a Lamb that appeared to have been slaughtered;"[40] the lion and the lamb, all in the same person.

> He had seven horns and seven eyes, which are the sevenfold Spirit of God sent out into all the earth.[41]

All the symbolism of the prophets must have collided in Yochanan's mind. His Master was represented by a lamb, but a lamb with seven (the number of perfection) powerful horns symbolizing rulership. Now he could see (understand) Zechariah's vision."..seven are the eyes of ADONAI that range about over all the earth…and the seven

39. Job 1:1
40. Rev 5:5–6
41. Rev. 5:6

lamps..."[42] His Master had truly been honored above all and now, the beloved disciple can see it just as Kefa was told when he asked Yeshua about Yochanan's future, "If I want him to stay on until I come, what is it to you? You, follow me!" Yochanan must have also remembered the words of his Master, "Yes! I tell you that there are some people standing here who will not experience death until they see the Son of Man coming in his Kingdom!"[43]

> He came and took the scroll out of the right hand of the One sitting on the throne.[44]

King David saw Messiah at the right hand of HaShem (Ps 110:1). For a long time, the terminology, "Your Right hand" ימינך referred to Messiah. The ceremony that must have been familiar to Yochanan continued:

> When he took the scroll, the four living beings and the twenty-four elders fell down in front of the Lamb. Each one held a harp and gold bowls filled with pieces of incense, which are the prayers of God's people.[45]

A Heavenly Service

Yochanan may have missed the recently destroyed Temple, but he was now part of the service of all services, the ritual of all rituals. He could see the twenty-four priestly leaders representing all of the Levites of Israel serving HaShem in the worship service of all worship services. They accompanied their songs of praise with harps; they sang songs of praise to HaShem for his victory over his enemies.[46] They also carried the prayers and the tears of all the persecuted disciples, of all those who were oppressed for righteousness' sake. What a comfort it must have been for Yochanan!

And they sang a new song.[47]

42. Zech 4:2, 10
43. Jn 21:22; Mt 16:28
44. Rev. 5:7
45. Rev. 5:8
46. Ps 144:9
47. Rev. 5:9

New songs were written at times of victory. Moshe sang a song celebrating Israel's narrow escape from the Egyptians. Deborah also wrote a song of victory. Against the backdrop of Roman persecutions, at a time when many were martyred, at a time when Yochanan himself was exiled to a labor camp with other political prisoners, he heard a song of victory in the courts of the heavenly throne. May our ears be always tuned to the heights of these songs of praise and victory, and not toward the dirges of the bleak abyss and its low earthly conditions! And what did this song say?

> You are worthy to take the scroll and break its seals; because you were slaughtered; at the cost of blood you ransomed for God persons from every tribe, language, people and nation. You made them into a kingdom for God to rule, cohanim to serve him; and they will rule over the earth.[48]

The Fall Feasts

After these things, I looked; and there before me was a door standing open in heaven. (Rev 5:11)

Yochanan has written messages to each of the seven congregations around the Aegean Sea. The purpose of these messages was to help these communities to prepare for future events and could be compared to the drill sergeant getting the troops ready for combat. Now Yochanan will receive the details of the mission at hand. He will be given "intelligence" to share with the congregations. Yochanan looks and sees that the "door of repentance" is opened.[49]

HaShem opens the door of the heavenlies. It's Rosh Hashanah, the time when each and every Jewish person around the world goes through introspection, apologizes to those they have hurt, restitutes borrowed items, sends donations and gifts, makes amends, and gives to the poor. The "door is opened" means there is room for repentance and acceptance. Our sages have taught us that this is what happens on this Memorial of Trumpets on the first day of the month of Tishri.[50] It is "auditing" time.

---

48. Rev. 5:9–10
49. Rev 3:20
50. Lev 23:24–25

HaShem looks down from the heavens and takes account of our lives. The Memorial of Trumpets is meant to remind us of the loud trumpets that blew on Mt. Horeb.[51]It reminds us of the giving of the Torah, by which we might live. It reminds us of our obligations toward the Torah as the great judgment day of Yom Kippur comes ten days later.[52]

It could be that Yochanan thought that was it. It was the end. The early believers indicate that they did feel that the return of Yeshua would happen in their day. Paul certainly spoke in those terms just as Yeshua did.[53] Talmudic teachings also teach about the coming of the Mashiach in the present tense. Here is a midrashic story that illustrates the point (my paraphrase). The story takes place during the Roman Empire:

> A rabbi met Elijah the prophet. The first question the bewildered Rabbi thought to ask was, "When does Mashiach come?" to which Elijah answered, "Today."[54]

Yochanan knew about the Fall festivals of Rosh Hashanah and Yom Kippur. He understood them as rehearsals for the coming of Mashiach in the World to Come. Judaism doesn't relate to eschatology with the idea of setting dates for certain events. The Torah forbids it. The idea is to prepare our hearts for these future events by being spiritually "audited" each year during the Fall Feasts. We know that Mashiach will come at that time, so we get ready for it each year. In any case, "to be ready" means to live godly lives, which are something we should be doing every day anyway, not just when he comes! He is like a parent who left the children for a few days with the care of the house and several chores to complete, but he is not telling them when he comes back. He can come back at any time to check on how they have been doing. In the same manner, we do not know when the Day of Mashiach is, so we should live as if it were h is "Today," as Yochanan did!

51. Exod 19:16
52. Lev 23:27–32
53. Mt 10:23
54. Referring to Psalm 95:7

CHAPTER 3
HEAVENLY SCROLL

- The First Seal: Caligula's Abomination
- The Second Seal: No More Peace
- The Third Seal: Oppression of The Poor
- The Fourth Seal: Death is Given Control
- The Fifth Seal: The Atoning Cries of The Martyrs
- The Message
- The Sixth Seal: The Day of Reckoning
- The Sealing of The Righteous
- Those in White Robes

The Lamb earned the right and privilege to open the precious and vital scroll that is in the hands of He Who sits on the Throne. From learning under the sages of his days, Yochanan knew that both the Name of Mashiach and Repentance were created before creation. He also knew that the Lamb was "slaughtered before the world was founded."[1] Yochanan finally understood that the events that transpired Rabbi Yeshua in Jerusalem were only for our human benefit: for us to witness an earthly revelation of these spiritual events.

The scope of HaShem's great plan is, and has always been, the establishment of the Kingdom of Heaven for all of humanity. Having witnessed Yeshua's modus operandi with their own eyes, the talmidim could better understand the dynamics which contribute to the establishment of the Kingdom. It would not be by the strength of armies; nor by wisdom, reason, or logic; nor by political or economic maneuvering. It would be by the humbling of ourselves and the laying down of our lives as HaShem's instruments; by living our daily lives

1. Rev 13:8; Prov 8: 22

accepting upon ourselves the fate of the Paschal Lamb who, though innocent, takes guilt upon himself.[2] Yochanan spent the rest of his life being and living that testimony to his Jewish brothers, as well as to the Gentiles around him. This rule of thumb comes in sharp contrast with the sheer military force by which worldly rulers, from the Egyptian Empire to today's Western world domination, establish their kingdoms on earth.

THE FIRST SEAL Caligula's Abomination

Yochanan watches as the glorious Lamb breaks the first seal. He will not know the detailed contents of the mysterious document until the seventh seal is broken. Like a chapter index in a book, each seal gives the apostle a quick overview of its contents. He is now about to see the spirits prevailing against the first century congregations. He is about to witness the dire warning spoken by future events. "I hope this will help them to see the seriousness of their calling and thus repent from their wrongdoing!" he hopes.

At the start of the prophetic vision Yeshua had told Yochanan, "... Write down what you see, both what is now, and what will happen afterwards..."[3] In his spiritual biography of the Master, and in these seven letters, the faithful scribe wrote what is now. He will write what will happen afterwards, as the vision unfolds before him.

> Next I watched as the Lamb broke the first of the seven seals, and I heard one of the four living beings say in a thundering voice, "Go!" I looked, and there in front of me was a white horse; its rider had a bow and was given a crown; and he rode off as a conqueror to conquer.[4]

Immediately, Yochanan remembers Zechariah's prophetic vision.[5] Yochanan lived at a time when the Roman Empire finally came to the zenith of its world conquest. Jerusalem and its Jewish Temple was one of the last frontiers of its world domination. Rome was riding

2. Zech 4:6
3. Rev 1:19
4. Rev 6:1–2
5. Zech 6:2–3

as a conqueror to conquer. From the Patmos labor camp where he was forced to remain, Yochanan witnessed firsthand the Pax Romana or, Roman "Peace on earth," that the Emperors boasted of: a thin whitewash that easily scratched and revealed its dark dynamics.

How could he forget! Ten years after the Master's ascension, Emperor Caligula tried to set up an idolatrous statue in the Jerusalem temple. The events were still fresh in the disciple's mind. Though Caligula's plan didn't succeed due to a miracle, it certainly reminded the whole Jewish community of believers of what Yeshua had told them a few days before his crucifixion. Yochanan was there when after a long day of teaching in the city, he, the other talmidim, and the Master, went to retire for the night on the Mount of Olives. It was then that, as they commented on the beauty of the Temple in the distance, that the Master told them, "You see all these? Yes! I tell you, they will be totally destroyed — not a single stone will be left standing!"[6] The talmidim were familiar with Daniel's prophecies, as well as the Talmudic teachings. They knew that troubles in Jerusalem and the destruction of the Temple would precede the establishment of the Messianic Kingdom by Mashiach. Equating the two together, they asked the Master, "Tell us ...when will these things happen? And what will be the sign that you are coming, and that the `olam hazeh is ending?"[7]

The establishment of the Messianic Kingdom is what they were living for; what they had given up everything for. This is what their understanding of "preaching the Gospel" was: to proclaim the arrival of the Messianic King who, in HaShem's name, will establish the Kingdom of God on earth in Jerusalem. They spoke of a physical kingdom, with a physical king.[8] They had welcomed him as such when he entered Jerusalem on a donkey, as Zechariah the prophet had foreseen.[9]

In answer to their questions, the Master gave the talmidim many signs: signs which they saw develop in their own days during the 40 years between his ascension and the destruction of the Temple. The

6. Mt 24:2
7. Mt 24:3
8. Isa 40:9; 52:7; 61:1
9. Zech 9:9

main sign the Master gave was, "When you see the abomination that causes desolation spoken about through the prophet Dani'el standing in the Holy Place (let the reader understand the allusion) ..."[10] The disciples understood that he was talking about events that happened less than two centuries ago; of the time when Emperor Antiochus Epiphanes set up an idolatrous statue in the Jewish Temple for people to worship. This provoked the Maccabean rebellion which they still celebrated yearly during the Festival of Chanukah in the winter. Yeshua answered the talmidim's questions concerning the future, by alluding to these past events. Many of the talmidim in those days were very anxious when Caligula's statue arrived at the shores of Caesarea and remained there for six months. Yochanan remembers that Chanukah was very special that year.

Yochanan was familiar with the prophecies of Daniel that indicated a world ruler who would bring the end of the Olam Hazeh, just before the establishment of Mashiach's Kingdom on earth, would come out of Rome.[11] He remembers the teachings of the Jewish sages about the "Counterfeit Mashiach" שקר משיח who would come to combat the real Mashiach. [12]As a Counterfeit Mashiach, he was to look like Mashiach and accomplish many things Mashiach is expected to accomplish to deceive the believers.

The time of the Roman Empire in the days of the talmidim was the last time there was peace all over the earth at one time. Through the false fear-enforced peace of the Pax Romana, one could almost say that the Roman Empire fulfilled the messianic promise of bringing universal peace. Yochanan was not deceived by this rider on a white horse trying to imitate the real Mashiach, whom he knew too well, and would also be coming on the scene riding a white horse.[13]

Yochanan remembered his Master speaking of false rulers, prophets, and shepherds. He compared them to hirelings to watch

10. Mt 24:15

11. Dan 7

12. The legendary name of this Counterfeit Mashiach is Armilus, a play on words with the name Romulus, who is said to be the founder of Rome. (Armilus appears frequently in the later Apocalyptic Midrashim, such as Midrash Va-Yosha, Sefer Zerubbavel, and Nistarot shel R. Shimon B. Yohai. He is also mentioned in the Targum Pseudo-Jonathan, and in the Targum Yerushalmi.)

13. Rev 19: 11–16

out for. He taught him how to recognize them: "a tree is known by its fruit."[14] A tree is not known by its appearance it is known by its fruits. It is not enough to wear a crown, have a bow, and ride a white horse like Mashiach. It is not enough to bring some sort of seeming peace like Mashiach will. Yochanan knew:

> He will judge between many peoples and arbitrate for many nations far away. Then they will hammer their swords into plow-blades and their spears into pruning-knives; nations will not raise swords at each other, and they will no longer learn war. Instead, each person will sit under his vine and fig tree, with no one to upset him, for the mouth of ADONAI-Tzva'ot has spoken. For all the peoples will walk, each in the name of its god; but we will walk in the name of ADONAI our God forever and ever.[15]

Peace and plenty for all? Rome didn't do that. Yochanan watches as his Master breaks the second seal.

THE SECOND SEAL No More Peace

> When he broke the second seal, I heard the second living being say, "Go!" Another horse went out, a red one; and its rider was given the power to take peace away from the earth and make people slaughter each other. He was given a great sword.[16]

The disciple watches as peace is now taken from the earth. From that time on, the world will never cease to be a battlefield somewhere at some time. Did he see the medieval and modern wars that still plague our world? The heart of man is truly given full sway. As the Master said, "Out of the heart come forth wicked thoughts, murder, adultery and other kinds of sexual immorality, theft, lies, slanders."[17]

---

14. Mt 12:33
15. Mic 4:3–5
16. Rev 6:3–4
17. Mt 15:19

THE THIRD SEAL Oppression of the Poor

> When he broke the third seal, I heard the third living being say, "Go!" I looked, and there in front of me was a black horse, and its rider held in his hand a pair of scales. Then I heard what sounded like a voice from among the four living beings say, "Two pounds of wheat for a day's wages! Six pounds of barley for the same price! But don't damage the oil or the wine!"[18]

Instead of peace and plenty for all, the black horse initiates a world of inequitable economic distribution. Yochanan sees a world where the price of bare necessities is exorbitant. The vision takes him to a society where the poor are oppressed by those who lend money for interest, a system which the Torah forbids as akin to oppressing the poor.[19] Yochanan knows that it is a sin which Mashiach will certainly address at the time appointed.[20] Even Ya'akov, the brother's Master said:

> Next, a word for the rich: weep and wail over the hardships coming upon you! Your riches have rotted, and your clothes have become moth-eaten; your gold and silver have corroded, and their corrosion will be evidence against you and will eat up your flesh like fire! This is the acharit-hayamim, and you have been storing up wealth! Listen! The wages you have fraudulently withheld from the workers who mowed your fields are calling out against you, and the outcries of those who harvested have reached the ears of ADONAI-Tzva'ot. You have led a life of luxury and self-indulgence here on earth — in a time of slaughter, you have gone on eating to your heart's content. You have condemned, you have murdered the innocent; they have not withstood you.[21]

Yochanan trembles for what the next seal may bring.

---

18. Rev 6:5–6

19. About lending to fellow Jews: Exod 22:25 - 26; Deut 23:19
A bout lending to non-Jews: Exod 22:21; 23:9
About lending in general: Mt 5:42

20. Deut 15:9

21. (Jas 5:1–6)

THE FOURTH SEAL Death is given Control

> When he broke the fourth seal, I heard the voice of the fourth living being say, "Go!" I looked, and there in front of me was a pallid, sickly-looking horse. Its rider's name was Death, and Sh'ol followed behind him. They were given authority to kill one-quarter of the world by war, by famine, by plagues and with the wild animals of the earth. (Rev 6:7–8)

In these four horses, Yochanan sees his world and its future. This is a useful message for the congregations. The key to their survival in such world was heeding the warnings they received in the letters. If they wanted to escape the judgment the world heaped upon itself, they needed to stay under the protection of Torah obedience. They needed to learn to stay away from the selfish ways of the world, just as the early Jewish believers of Jerusalem did.[22] Yochanan remembered the words of his co-apostle Paul to the Thessalonian congregations as preparation against those troubling days:

> Therefore, encourage each other, and build each other up — just as you are doing. We ask you, brothers, to respect those who are working hard among you, those who are guiding you in the Lord and confronting you in order to help you change. Treat them with the highest regard and love because of the work they are doing. Live at peace among yourselves; but we urge you, brothers, to confront those who are lazy, your aim being to help them change, to encourage the timid, to assist the weak, and to be patient with everyone. See that no one repays evil for evil; on the contrary, always try to do good to each other, indeed, to everyone. Always be joyful. Pray regularly. In everything give thanks, for this is what God wants from you who are united with the Messiah Yeshua. (1Th 5:11–18)

Yochanan watches as Yeshua breaks the fifth seal.

22. Acts 2:44-45; 4:32

THE FIFTH SEAL The Atoning Cries of the Martyrs — The Message

> When the Lamb broke the fifth seal, I saw underneath the altar the souls of those who had been put to death for proclaiming the Word of God, that is, for bearing witness.[23]

How Yochanan weeps as he sees his friends, his brothers, and sisters martyred in the name of the cruel Roman law, an action he refers to as *Kiddush HaShem* קידוש השם: "Sanctifying the Name of HaShem." He saw rabbis, priests, and Yeshua's talmidim executed for challenging the decree to worship the Emperor, a rule that neither the talmidim nor any other Jew could follow.

Gentile brothers and sisters were in a different predicament. Those who held the status of Roman citizens, like Paul, had protective rights under Roman law. They could compromise and avoid martyrdom. But if they were seen observing Jewish festivals and dietary laws, they were exposed as traitors to the Empire, having adopted the Jewish religion. The Romans didn't care much for genealogical descent or Jewish theology. In their eyes, if you worshiped like a Jew and if you ate like a Jew, you were a Jew and therefore should be exposed as one who refused to worship the Emperor. For these Gentile disciples, a small compromise could change everything. A small tweaking and twisting of Paul's writings concerning dietary laws, Shabbat, festival observances, and circumcision, could get them off the Roman hook. Creative teachers then re-interpreted the words of the apostle as saying that they did not have to observe these Jewish rituals, which allowed them to blend with the Roman population.

In any case, at the opening of the fifth seal, Yochanan could see some of the people he knew. Maybe he saw Ya'akov his brother, who had been arrested and put to death by Herod Agrippa's sword. Maybe he could see the other Ya'akov, Yeshua's brother, who had also been martyred, stoned at the hands of Sadducean High Priest Hanan ben Hanana. Maybe Yochanan even caught a glimpse of Peter and Paul who had been executed under Emperor Caligula. He must have seen

23. (Rev 6:9)

all those whom the writer of the letter to Hebrews compared to the prophets of old, saying:

> What more should I say? There isn't time to tell about Gid`on, Barak, Shimshon, Yiftach, David, Sh'mu'el and the prophets; who, through trusting, conquered kingdoms, worked righteousness, received what was promised, shut the mouths of lions, quenched the power of fire, escaped the edge of the sword, had their weakness turned to strength, grew mighty in battle and routed foreign armies. Women received back their dead resurrected; other people were stretched on the rack and beaten to death, refusing to be ransomed, so that they would gain a better resurrection. Others underwent the trials of being mocked and whipped, then chained and imprisoned. They were stoned, sawed in two, murdered by the sword; they went about clothed in sheepskins and goatskins, destitute, persecuted, mistreated, wandering about in deserts and mountains, living in caves and holes in the ground! The world was not worthy of them! All of these had their merit attested because of their trusting. Nevertheless, they did not receive what had been promised, because God had planned something better that would involve us, so that only with us would they be brought to the goal.[24]

These martyrs were under the altar. Their blood had been spilled for proclaiming the Word of God, that is, for bearing witness. Yochanan saw their innocent blood in the image of the innocent animals, whose blood was spilled twice a day, at the bottom of the altar to provide atonement for the children of Israel. Like Abel's blood, the blood of these innocent righteous people killed, for the sake of their testimony, is innocent and therefore provides atonement for others. Yochanan hears their prayers for their brothers and sisters:

> They cried out in a loud voice, "Sovereign Ruler, HaKadosh, the True One, how long will it be before you judge the people living on earth and avenge our blood?[25]

24. Heb 11:32–40
25. Rev 6:10

Yochanan must have been proud of his brothers and sisters. As is commanded in the Torah, they do not seek to avenge themselves, but patiently wait for HaShem to avenge them.

> Each of them was given a white robe; and they were told to wait a little longer, until the full number of their fellow-servants should be reached, of their brothers who would be killed, just as they had been.[26]

The Message

Yochanan understands the message. Persecutions will not be over for a while. Things will continue to be as it was in the days of the faithful emissary on the Isle of Patmos when the early believers are challenging the Roman Emperor's demands of worship. Rome will continue persecuting the Jews, believers and unbelievers alike, until the time on the consummation of the Messianic Age. "Will my message reach the generations of tomorrow?" he wonders. Yochanan at that moment must have remembered the words of his Master when he taught about the days preceding the fulfillment of the Messianic Age:

> For there will be trouble then worse than there has ever been from the beginning of the world until now, and there will be nothing like it again! Indeed, if the length of this time had not been limited, no one would survive; but for the sake of those who have been chosen, its length will be limited.[27]

THE SIXTH SEAL The Day of Reckoning

> Then I watched as he broke the sixth seal, and there was a great earthquake, the sun turned black as sackcloth worn in mourning, and the full moon became blood-red. The stars fell from heaven to earth just as a fig tree drops its figs when shaken by a strong wind.[28]

26. Rev 6:11
27. Mt 24: 21-22
28. Rev 6:12–14

Yochanan sees the answers to the prayers of the righteous martyrs. As in the days of the Exodus from Egypt, HaShem will rise and save his people from the hands of the cruel oppressor. In Yochanan's ears, these words might again echo the teachings of his Master:

> For when the Son of Man does come, it will be like lightning that flashes out of the east and fills the sky to the western horizon. Wherever there's a dead body, that's where you find the vultures. But immediately following the trouble of those times, the sun will grow dark, the moon will stop shining, the stars will fall from the sky, and the powers in heaven will be shaken. Then the sign of the Son of Man will appear in the sky, all the tribes of the Land will mourn, and they will see the Son of Man coming on the clouds of heaven with tremendous power and glory.[29]

The vision continues unfolding:

> The sky receded like a scroll being rolled up, and every mountain and island was moved from its place. Then the earth's kings, the rulers, the generals, the rich and the mighty — indeed, everyone, slave and free — hid himself in caves and among the rocks in the mountains, and said to the mountains and rocks, "Fall on us, and hide us from the face of the One sitting on the throne and from the fury of the Lamb! For the Great Day of their fury has come, and who can stand?"[30]

The old disciple remembered the teachings that the Messianic Age will be a time of reversal of fortunes, a time when the ruler will be the servant and the servant the ruler; where he who was rich in this age will be impoverished in the next, and vice-versa. He remembered the Master's teachings about Lazarus and the rich man. In the parable Abraham says to the rich man:

> Son, remember that when you were alive, you got the good things while he got the bad; but now he gets his consolation here, while you are the one in agony.[31]

29. Mt 24:27–30
30. Rev 6:14–17
31. Lu 16:25

> After this, I saw four angels standing at the four corners of the earth, holding back the four winds of the earth, so that no wind would blow on the land, on the sea or on any tree.[32]

Rabbi Yeshua had already warned Yochanan and the other talmidim that great destruction was at hand. The Master warned of a destruction that would cripple the economies of the world. It was not a question of if, it was a question of when. Already, due to the Imperial persecutions against Judaism, the very counter-culture nature of the messianic congregations who obeyed the Master, caused the talmidim to live in a constant state of preparation for the worst. In view of these coming days, through the teachings of Paul and that of the others shlichim[33], they had to learn to get over their personal problems and issues with each other. They had to learn to get over their selfishness and share. They knew that if they didn't "hang together," they would surely "hang separately." Paul, Kefa, and Ya'akov wrote many articles about life in preparation for the turbulent times preceding the return of Yeshua. They told the disciples everywhere that it was imperative to their survival to clean their hearts of hatred, pride, selfishness, laziness, bigotry, revelry, disobedience, anger, and of all these things that eat at our virtues and unity.

The Sealing of the Righteous

> I saw another angel coming up from the east with a seal from the living God, and he shouted to the four angels who had been given power to harm the land and the sea, "Do not harm the land or the sea or the trees until we have sealed the servants of our God on their foreheads!" (Rev 7:2–3)

Yochanan did not want to scare the congregations into "behaving." He wanted to encourage them to serve HaShem out of love. His style of leadership was truly exceptional. Though he at times was frustrated with some of the leaders' inability to monitor congregants, he would put his own life at risk to rescue the wayward with loving tears of

32. (Rev 7:1)

33. For example, 1 Thes 5

compassion. Here is the report concerning a young congregant who went astray into a life of banditry after Yochanan had given charge of him to an Ephesus leader.

> The Apostle rent his clothes, and beating his head with great lamentation, he said, "A fine guard I left for a brother's soul! But let a horse be brought me, and let someone show me the way." He rode away ... just as he was, and coming to the place, he was taken prisoner by the robbers' outpost. He, however, neither fled nor made entreaty, but cried out, "For this did I come; lead me to your captain." The latter, meanwhile, was waiting, armed as he was. But when he recognized [Yochanan] approaching, he turned in shame to flee. But [Yochanan], forgetting his age, pursued him with all his might, crying out, "Why, my son, do you flee from me, your own father, unarmed, aged? Pity me, my son; fear not; you have still hope of life. I will give account to [Mashiach] for you. If need be, I will willingly endure your death as the [Master] suffered death for us. For you will I give up my life. Stand, believe; [Mashiach] has sent me." And he, when he heard, first stopped and looked down; then he threw away his arms, and then trembled and wept bitterly. And when the old man approached, he embraced him, making confession with lamentations as he was able, [immersing] himself a second time with tears, and concealing only his right hand. But [Yochanan], pledging himself, and assuring him on oath that he would find forgiveness with the [Mashiach], besought him, fell upon his knees, kissed his right hand itself as if now purified by repentance, and led him back to the [congregation of believers]. And making intercession for him with copious prayers, and struggling together with him in continual fastings, and subduing his mind by various utterances, he did not depart, as they say, until he had restored him to the [congregation], furnishing a great example of true repentance and a great proof of regeneration, a trophy of a visible resurrection. [34]

Yochanan had learned from his Master Yeshua that humility had more power to win a brother than loud harassing condescension, and humiliation. He was familiar with the old Davidic statement:

וַתִּתֶּן-לִי, מָגֵן יִשְׁעֶךָ: וִימִינְךָ תִסְעָדֵנִי; וְעַנְוַתְךָ תַרְבֵּנִי

34. Ecclesiastical History 3:23, Eusebius

> You give me your shield, which is salvation, your right hand holds me up, your humility [or condescension] makes me great.35

Yochanan was now able to reassure the people. He would tell them that nothing will happen until the chosen are sealed.

> I heard how many were sealed — 144,000 from every tribe of the people of Isra'el: From the tribe of Y'hudah 12,000 were sealed, from the tribe of Re'uven 12,000, from the tribe of Gad 12,000, from the tribe of Asher 12,000, from the tribe of Naftali 12,000, from the tribe of M'nasheh 12,000, from the tribe of Shim`on 12,000, from the tribe of Levi 12,000, from the tribe of Yissakhar 12,000, from the tribe of Z'vulun 12,000, from the tribe of Yosef 12,000, from the tribe of Binyamin 12,000.36

Yochanan probably saw a familiar pattern. There was such a time in the history of Israel when HaShem sent a keruv to apply a seal of protection on all the citizens of Jerusalem who opposed the abomination practiced in the Holy city:

> ADONAI said to him [to the keruv], "Go throughout the city, through all Yerushalayim, and put a mark on the foreheads of the men who are sighing and crying over all the disgusting practices that are being committed in it."37

Ya'akov, the brother of the Master, was known for his intercessory prayers for Israel, but Yochanan had also certainly cried and wept over the fate of the Jewish believers of his day. They were caught between the Roman government's persecution of Jews, the harassment of the Sadducee-influenced Israelites, and the Gentile believers who rejected and harassed them. At this time of the vision, Yochanan sees some good news. He reassures them that no matter what happens to them in the earthly reality, their heavenly fate was sealed. Twelve thousand from each tribe, or 144.000 Jewish believers, would be given HaShem's seal of protection. As Yochanan is shown later, they will eventually rejoice in a song of victory:

35. Ps 18:35
36. Rev 7:4–8
37. Ezek 9:4

> They were singing a new song before the throne and before the four living beings and the elders, and no one could learn the song except the 144,000 who have been ransomed from the world. These are the ones who have not defiled themselves with women, for they are virgins; they follow the Lamb wherever he goes; they have been ransomed from among humanity as first fruits for God and the Lamb; on their lips no lie was found — they are without defect.[38]

Not only do these receive a seal of protection, but they serve as first fruits. Just as in farming and agriculture, the whole flock or harvest is sanctified through the offering of a firstborn or of a first fruit omer, so the whole Jewish nation is sanctified by way of the redemption of this sealed first fruit. Yochanan was probably elated at these words of hope. He probably remembered Paul's words on the issue.39 "Now, if the hallah offered as first fruits is holy, so is the whole loaf. And if the root is holy, so are the branches."40 Yochanan continues watching. He sees before him:

> A huge crowd, too large for anyone to count, from every nation, tribe, people and language.[41]

This reminded Yochanan of a very big principle in HaShem's economy: When Abraham rescued Lot, he also freed the people from Sodom and Gomorrah who had been taken as prisoners. When Israel left Egypt, a great multitude from all nations followed them. When HaShem delivered the Jews from Haman's clutches, many Babylonians converted to Judaism. When he delivers his people, he includes others from the nations.

In the vision of the 144.000 sealed Messianic Jews, the Israelites are represented by their own first fruit, and after that, Israel stands as the first fruit for the rest of humanity. As Paul rightly mentioned concerning Israel:

38. Rev 14:3–5
39. Exod 34:19; Num 3:12–13
40. Rom 11:16 see appendix 1
41. Rev 7:9

> Moreover, if their stumbling is bringing riches to the world — that is, if Isra'el's being placed temporarily in a condition less favored than that of the Gentiles is bringing riches to the latter — how much greater riches will Isra'el in its fullness bring them![42]

Yochanan understood the old teachings more fully. He rejoiced as he saw the 144.000 Jewish believers alongside with those from the nations giving praise and glory to HaShem using a familiar liturgical doxology:

> Standing in front of the throne and in front of the Lamb, dressed in white robes and holding palm branches in their hands; and they shouted, "Victory to our God, who sits on the throne, and to the Lamb!"[43]

People of all tribes and nations, having come in their white clothes for the fall festivals, are now gathered together for Sukkot and waving their lulavs at the festival of Tabernacles. At the beautiful sight, Yochanan remembers Zechariah:

> Finally, everyone remaining from all the nations that came to attack Yerushalayim will go up every year to worship the king, ADONAI-Tzva'ot, and to keep the festival of Sukkot.[44]

Yochanan even witnesses the angels involvement:

> All the angels stood around the throne, the elders and the four living beings; they fell face down before the throne and worshipped God, saying, "Amen!" Praise and glory, wisdom and thanks, honor and power and strength belong to our God forever and ever! "Amen!"[45]

So far, except for the time when he cried because he thought no one could open the book, Yochanan had been a silent presence; a quiet observer of what was unfolding in front of him. Suddenly, someone from that spiritual realm addresses him with a question.

---

42. Rom 11:12
43. Rev 7:10
44. Rev 7:10
45. Rev 7:11–12

Those in White Robes

> These people dressed in white robes — who are they, and where are they from?[46]

Although Yochanan can see that these were people from all nations, he had learned that in this earthly realm ... we see obscurely in a mirror and ...know partly.[47] So in his typical humility, he does not assume knowledge, but answers:

> Sir, you know. Then he told me… [48]

Yochanan's humility pays off. Concerning these people in white robes, the elder tells him:

> These are the people who have come out of the Great Persecution. They have washed their robes and made them white with the blood of the Lamb. That is why they are before God's throne.[49]

This is good news and bad news. These people in white robes are accepted in the presence of HaShem's throne, which is the highest privilege a person could ask for. Yochanan knows that even when the Temple was standing, only the appointed High-Priest was allowed near the Ark in the Holy of Holies, and only at the appointed time of Yom Kippur. Yochanan remembers Aaron's sons, Nadab and Abihu, who disobeyed the Tabernacle's protocol and paid for it with their lives. When the High-Priest came in front of the Ark, he did not wear his glorious priestly garments. He came in the humility of a simple linen garment. Now, Yochanan sees all these in white linen robes in front to the thrones just as if they were high-priests. "How beautiful," Yochanan thinks as he remembers the promises of priesthood given to Moshe about Israel, and those of Kefa to the persecuted Roman congregation:

---

46. Rev 7:11–12
47. 1 Cor 13:12
48. Rev 7:14
49. Rev 7:14–15

> But you are a chosen people, the King's cohanim, a holy nation, a people for God to possess! Why? In order for you to declare the praises of the One who called you out of darkness into his wonderful light. [50]

Day and night they serve him in his Temple.[51]

Yochanan was there when Yeshua asked the question, Now won't God grant justice to his chosen people who cry out to him day and night? Is he delaying long over them?[52] He knew then that by talking about those who cry out to him day and night, the Master had knowingly made allusions to, I have posted watchmen on your walls, Yerushalayim; they will never fall silent, neither by day nor by night. You who call on ADONAI, give yourselves no rest.[53] These priests in white robes serve HaShem day and night. They perpetually cry and intercede to him for the sake of their brethren on earth. The elder continues:

> They will never again be hungry, they will never again be thirsty, the sun will not beat down on them, nor will any burning heat. "For the Lamb at the center of the throne will shepherd them, will lead them to springs of living water, and God will wipe every tear from their eyes."[54]

Isaiah's prophecy comes to Yochanan's mind, the prophecy of a day when Isra'el, will be neither hungry nor thirsty; neither scorching wind nor sun will strike them; for he who has mercy on them will lead them and guide them to springs of water.[55] Now, Yochanan waits for the opening of the seventh seal.

---

50. 1 Peter 2:9
51. Rev 7:15
52. Lu 18:7
53. Isa 62:6
54. Rev 7:16–17
55. Isa 49:10

CHAPTER 4
SEVEN SHOFARS OF DOOM

- The Breaking of the Seventh Seal
  - The Seven Shofars
  - An Angel at the Altar of Incense
  - The Voice of the First Shofar
  - The Voice of the Second, Third, and Fourth Shofar
  - The Voice of the Fifth Shofar
  - The Voice of the Sixth Shofar
- The Master Introduces the Seventh Shofar
  - Yochanan Eats the Scroll!
  - Vision of a Third Temple.
  - Two Witnesses.
  - The Earthquake
  - The Voice of the Seventh Shofar
  - The Temple Opens to Display the Ark
- Miriam in the Sky with the Dragon/Tanin!
- The Dragon, the Beast … and the other beast
- The Lamb and the 144.000
- Messages of Good news
- The Harvest

The Breaking of the Seventh Seal

Six seals are now broken. As each of them loosens the precious scroll a little more, Yochanan sees the world of his days with its hypocritical pretenses of peace, and its openly hateful wars, a result of its selfish greed. Yochanan also gets a glimpse of the horrendous illnesses that plague the earth.

The sixth seal brings the elderly apostle to a preview of the awesome days preceding the establishment of the Kingdom of Messiah on earth.

It is with great joy that he notices the believers from the twelve tribes standing as the "first fruit of humanity." Yochanan waits expectantly for the opening of the seventh seal, which will finally release the prophetic content of the mysterious scroll. It will be the ...what will happen afterwards part of the message from Yeshua.[1]

Yochanan is in a heightened state of suspense.

> When the Lamb broke the seventh seal, there was silence in heaven for what seemed like half an hour.[2]

From the time of his arrival in the throne room, Yochanan is surrounded by the sound of the continuous praises and laments: the praises coming from the four beasts around the throne, and the laments of the martyred saints asking for vindication. Silence now fills the air. This silence brings him great nostalgia as he remembers the Amidah עמדה, the thirty minute silent prayer that formed a major portion of the twice daily Temple and synagogue services. The breaking of the seventh seal reveals a two-part document. The first part punctuated by the voice of seven shofars, and the second, by seven bowls of wrath. Yochanan watches intently.

The Seven Shofars

> And I saw seven angels who stand before God, and they were given seven shofars.[3]

Yochanan, though Galilean, spent a great deal of time in Jerusalem. He was familiar with the sound of the seven daily trumpet blasts. How could he forget the special times when he and the other disciples would wait for the first blast at the opening of the Temple gates?[4] By the end of the morning, he would have heard three more blasts, and three more by the end of the day. How beautiful did the voice of these seven shofars sound to him! Was he about to hear them again? In the

1. Rev 1:19
2. Rev 8:1
3. Rev 8:2
4. Acts 2:42,46

theme and backdrop of the fall festivals, the view of the seven shofars in the hands of the seven angels who stood before HaShem might have sent shivers down Yochanan's spine.

Shofars are usually blown to announce happy times, such as Shabbats and other festivals, but a shofar blown at an unexpected time is like a comet in the night sky. It is a sign of impending doom, natural disaster, or war. What was the announcement to be made?

An Angel at the Altar of Incense

> Another angel came and stood at the altar with a gold incense-bowl, and he was given a large quantity of incense to add to the prayers of all God's people on the gold altar in front of the throne…[5]

Yochanan was familiar with the Temple's structure. He was elated to be privy to what Moshe saw on Mount Horeb. Though not a priest (who has access to the first chamber of the Temple), Yochanan knew about the incense altar that stood before the curtain of the Holy of Holies, of the Kadosh Hak'doshim,קדוש הקדושים the second chamber of the Tabernacle where the Holy Ark dwells. From where he stands, Yochanan can see the original altar opposite of HaShem. He sees the angel who receives incense to offer on it. The old apostle remembers the yearly Yom Kippur service. He remembers the High Priest following, according to what was commanded Aaron: He is to take a censer full of burning coals from the altar before ADONAI and, with his hands full of ground, fragrant incense, bring it inside the curtain.[6]

> The smoke of the incense went up with the prayers of God's people from the hand of the angel before God.[7]

The marveling disciple watches as the smoke of the incense, which represents the prayers of HaShem's people, goes straight into the nostrils of the Ancient of Days whom we call: "Abba אבא שבשמים Shebashamayim, Our Father who is in heaven." More incense was

5. Rev 8:3
6. Lev 16:12
7. Rev 8:4

given, which tells us of the increased intensity of the prayers of those from earth. The time of Yochanan under Emperor Domitian was a time of intense persecution. As HaShem had heard the cry of his children in Egypt, he was now hearing the cry of his children in the lands around the Aegean Sea.

> Then the angel took the incense-bowl, filled it with fire from the altar and threw it down onto the earth; and there followed peals of thunder, voices, flashes of lightning and an earthquake.[8]

In addition to the sound of the shofars, the scene of Mt. Horeb with its thunder, voices, flashes of lightning, and earthquake is replayed all over again for Yochanan. The announcement is simple. As HaShem had been faithful to vindicate, deliver, and lead his children from the unjust slavery of Egypt, he will also vindicate, deliver, and lead his children from Roman oppression.

Yochanan can see now. The hour of vindication and retribution, the hour of justice, has come. The time has come for all the wrongs of the earth to be at long last rectified, and for all injustices committed towards those created in HaShem's image, especially those injustices committed in his Name, to come before him. The hour has come

- for all those who have been oppressed by man's greedy and selfish economic systems;
- for all those who have suffered under political, racial, or religious bigotry;
- for all those whose lands have been taken or dominated by the mighty and powerful;
- for all the victims of racial or economic slavery, to have "their day in court."

As the angel throws down the bowl of incense, HaShem throws the prayers of the persecuted to the earth. Now the world can have a serious look at its cruel and horrific governments since the day he has

8. Rev 8:5

appropriated to himself the right to govern in the days of Nimrod, at the time of the Tower of Babel.

Justice and vindication has also come for the disciples of the Master who, when reviled, reviled not again; when mocked, kept their quiet.[9] For all those who aspired "to a better fatherland, a heavenly one, and those who, were stretched on the rack and beaten to death, refusing to be ransomed, so that they would gain a better resurrection;"[10].

The apostle who wrote these words about the Jewish believers in Israel, many of whom Yochanan must have known, invokes that, "The world was not worthy of them! All of these had their merit attested because of their trusting. Yochanan could now see that, as the apostle claimed, they did not receive what had been promised, because God had planned something better that would involve us, so that only with us would they be brought to the goal."[11]

True disciples of Yeshua live in that assurance, that he is their justice. They not only believe, but they know that the Day of the Great Rectification of all wrongs is at hand! "Vengeance and payback are mine for the time when their foot slips; for the day of their calamity is coming soon, their doom is rushing upon them" he said.[12] At that time, he will avenge the blood of all those who died for the sake of HaShem. Abel; all the prophets; the early disciples; all the Jews who died in persecutions, including those in the Holocaust and those of the nations who died for the sake of resisting the influence of the pagan Empires in order to follow the Torah.

Yochanan can see there and then that HaShem has not forgotten his children, his people in all these congregations around the Aegean Sea. Though at times seemingly absent, as in the days of Moshe, Esther, Daniel, and the Maccabees, HaShem is present and involved in the fate of his people.

The awesome, unexpected shofars are getting ready to blow. The blowing of the shofar at Yom Kippur announces the year of Jubilee. For some, this advent is an advent of good news. The

9. Deut 19:6
10. Heb 11:16–35
11. Heb 11:39-40
12. Deut 32:35

once every fifty years Day of Jubilee launches the return of many promises. It brings the freeing of all slaves, the remission of all debts, and the returning of all lands, even if the borrower did not have the money to pay his debt. In this system, HaShem ensures the rich do not get too rich and forget him, and the poor do not get too poor and curse him.

For others, at this time of the fall festivals, these shofars may seem like an omen of impending doom. They represent the cries of a vengeful redeemer coming to the rescue and deliverance of his own. As Abraham delivered righteous Lot from Sodom,[13] and as HaShem protected the children of Israel from the plagues poured on Egypt,[14] when judgment is exercised on the world, his servants are sealed with a divine seal of protection.

The Voice of the First Shofar

> Now the seven angels with the seven shofars prepared to sound them. The first one sounded his shofar; and there came hail and fire mingled with blood, and it was thrown down upon the earth.[15]

Yochanan envisions the same God at work as the one who liberated his people from Egypt. The Passover Seder reciting of the plagues probably goes through his mind with the seventh plague in the forefront.

The Voices of the Second, Third, and Fourth Shofars

> A third of the earth was burned up, a third of the trees were burned up, and all green grass was burned up. The second angel sounded his shofar, and what looked like an enormous blazing mountain was hurled into the sea. A third of the sea turned to blood, a third of the living creatures in the sea died, and a third of the ships were destroyed. The third angel sounded his shofar;

13. 2 Peter 2:7
14. Exod 7:12
15. Rev 8:6–7

> and a great star, blazing like a torch, fell from the sky onto a third of the rivers and onto the springs of water. The name of the star was "Bitterness," and a third of the water became bitter, and many people died from the water that had been turned bitter. The fourth angel sounded his shofar; and a third of the sun was struck, also a third of the moon and a third of the stars; so that a third of them were darkened, the day had a third less light, and the night likewise.[16]

The voices of these first four shofars are directed at the environment. The cataclysmic events they announce will inevitably negatively affect the life of the people on the earth.

Looking back at HaShem's redemptive works in the days of Moshe, Yochanan anticipates the coming scenario. From the ancient texts, he remembers when HaShem offered rescue from the last terrible plague as well as freedom from Egyptian oppression. The offer was made indiscriminately, regardless of someone's goodness, wickedness, or biological descent. All they had to do was follow the Mosaic instruction concerning the lamb, the last dinner, and the time of exit.

When universal judgment comes, all are punished, guilty and innocent alike. Even those who are innocent such as children or people who never were given a chance to know. Yochanan understands that the time of redemption is a precious cosmic moment when all get a chance, regardless of whether they deserve it or not. Yochanan hears a screeching sound from the sky:

> Then I looked, and I heard a lone vulture give a loud cry, as it flew in mid-heaven, "Woe! Woe! Woe to the people living on earth, because of the remaining blasts from the three angels who have yet to sound their shofars!"[17]

Yochanan sees a lone *nesher* נשר, or vulture. He remembers when his beloved Master spoke of vultures as he expounded on the awesome days to come. He remembers that time in the cool of the day, two

16. Rev 8:6–12
17. Rev 8:13

days before the Passover. After spending the whole day teaching at the Temple, the Master and his disciples walked back to the Mount of Olives for the evening. Being from Galilee, they enjoyed the scenic view of the Temple buildings. The Master then commented that from it, not one stone would be left standing on another.

The disciples who had studied the Torah equated the destruction of the Temple with the imminent coming of the Kingdom of Heaven; the time when Israel would be restored as a sovereign nation, with Messiah on its throne, ruling the world from Jerusalem. This was, after all, the message that both the Master and Yochanan the Immerser had preached, Repent, for the Kingdom of Heaven is at hand! At one point in the discussion, the Master said:

> Also, at the time of the Son of Man, it will be just as it was at the time of Noach. People ate and drank, and men and women married, right up until the day Noach entered the ark; then the flood came and destroyed them all. Likewise, as it was in the time of Lot — people ate and drank, bought and sold, planted and built; but the day Lot left S'dom, fire and sulfur rained down from heaven and destroyed them all. That is how it will be on the day the Son of Man is revealed. On that day, if someone is on the roof with his belongings in his house, he must not go down to take them away. Similarly, if someone is in the field, he must not turn back —remember Lot's wife! Whoever aims at preserving his own life will lose it, but whoever loses his life will stay alive. I tell you, on that night there will be two people in one bed — one will be taken and the other left behind. There will be two women grinding grain together — one will be taken and the other left behind." ["Two men will be in a field — one will be taken and the other left behind."] They asked him, "Where, Lord?" He answered, "Wherever there's a dead body, that's where the vultures gather."[18]

This mention of "vultures gathering," mixed with the "time of Noah," and that of Sodom, was both telling and descriptive. Yochanan knew that Yeshua used a theme from the prophet Isaiah in his answer. He

18. Luke 17:26–37

could remember the eighth-century BCE prophet's description of HaShem's vengeance against his enemies at the end of this age. A great destruction occurs on a famous battlefield. Carcasses lie in the sun to rot at the mercy of vultures. Ezekiel concurred with that vision,[19] and Yochanan will see it first-hand.[20]

Yeshua connected this prophetic picture with that of the days of Noah and of Sodom. In those days, scavengers cleaned the land and the waters from the dead carcasses that resulted from HaShem's judgments. In those days, Yeshua said to his disciples, "There will be two women grinding grain together — one will be taken and the other left behind. Two men will be in a field — one will be taken and the other left behind."[21]

Then the disciples asked him, "Where, Lord?" In other words, "Those who are taken, where are they taken to?," "Wherever there's a dead body, that's where the vultures gather," the Master answered. The ones who are "taken" are the ones who died and have become prey to the vultures. The ones left behind are the ones who were saved from the destruction, the ones who, like Noah, Lot, and his daughters, are alive on earth to continue the establishment of the Kingdom of HaShem on earth, as will the ones who are alive when Mashiach comes in his glory. Yochanan watches the scavenger in his macabre circular dance as he anticipates a soon coming feast. The screeching sounds that accompany his dance tell of the destruction announced by the three last shofars.

Yochanan hears the voice of the fifth shofar.

The Voice of the Fifth Shofar

> The fifth angel sounded his shofar; and I saw a star that had fallen out of heaven onto the earth, and he was given the key to the shaft leading down to the Abyss.[22]

19. Ez 39:11
20. Rev 19:17–18
21. Lu 17:35–36
22. Rev 9:1

Yochanan sees an angel falling. This angel receives the key to a shaft leading down to the abyss of the sea. Yochanan will see this angel again.[23]

> He opened the shaft of the Abyss, and there went up smoke from the shaft like the smoke of a huge furnace; the sun was darkened, and the sky too, by the smoke from the shaft. Then out of the smoke onto the earth came locusts, and they were given power like the power scorpions have on earth.[24]

When Yochanan sees the smoke coming out of the shaft and the locusts, he remembers Joel's oracle:

> A day of darkness and gloom, a day of clouds and thick darkness! Like blackness there is spread upon the mountains a great and powerful people; their like has never been before, nor will be again after them through the years of all generations. Fire devours before them, and behind them a flame burns. The land is like the garden of Eden before them, but behind them a desolate wilderness, and nothing escapes them. Their appearance is like the appearance of horses, and like war horses they run. As with the rumbling of chariots, they leap on the tops of the mountains, like the crackling of a flame of fire devouring the stubble, like a powerful army drawn up for battle. Before them peoples are in anguish; all faces grow pale. Like warriors they charge; like soldiers they scale the wall. They march each on his way; they do not swerve from their paths.[25]

Yochanan ponders. The Valley of Megiddo in his beloved Galilee has been the battlefield of many armed conflicts. As he studied the prophets, he often tried to visualize the prophecies spoken by Joel. He could only imagine those of Gideon's against the Midianites, the Amalekites, and the children of the East. He remembers King Saul leading Israel into victory against the Philistines. He sometimes wonders if the last battles of Messiah that he learned about would be fought in this valley!

23. Rev 20:1
24. Rev 9:2–3
25. Joel 2:2–7

> What the cutting locust left, the swarming locust has eaten. What the swarming locust left, the hopping locust has eaten, and what the hopping locust left, the destroying locust has eaten.[26]

Like in the days of the plagues of Egypt, Yochanan sees an army resembling a plague of locusts. Swarms of locusts come and devour all in their path, leaving lush lands like scorched earth behind them. Yochanan sees this great army. An army under the command of one called in Hebrew *Abaddon* אבדון that the Master himself releases into battle. Again, Yochanan is reminded of the Rosh-Hashanah/ Yom Kippur synagogue liturgy, which includes the reading of Joel's prophecy of the locusts.

Yochanan is relieved when he hears the instructions given to the locusts:

> They were instructed not to harm the grass on the earth, any green plant or any tree, but only the people who did not have the seal of God on their foreheads.[27]

One hundred forty-four thousand, twelve thousand from each of the tribes of Israel, have been sealed with the seal of HaShem and that of the Lamb, as well as a great multitude from all nations. This army of "locusts" is directed by HaShem against those who did not have his seal on their foreheads.

Again, Yochanan remembers the stories of Egypt as they are told at every Passover seder. Not only did the legions of locusts that came to devour the ripened crops of the Egyptians come to his mind, but also the many plagues that were directed only at the Egyptians, while the city of Goshen, where the Israelites lived, was spared.

The old disciple also remembers Amos, who received visions of the future. The prophet from Tekoa saw HaShem at the head of an army compared to locusts. This swarm of locusts came to punish Israel, but in the end, HaShem heard Amos' desperate plea and repented from the evil he was going to do to Israel.[28]

26. Joel 1:4
27. Rev 9:4
28. Amos 7:1–3

Yochanan also knew that in the prophecies of Joel, HaShem answered the prayers of the High Priest for Israel and said, "No, I will take the northerner away, far away from you, and drive him to a land that is waste and barren; with his vanguard toward the eastern sea and his rearguard toward the western sea, his stench and his rottenness will rise, because he has done great things."[29] In the prophecy, HaShem throws the attacker into the Dead Sea and into the Mediterranean Sea, where he will rot.

HaShem calls this army of locusts, the "Northerner" as he seems to have come from the North. The invader coming from the north is an often-recurring theme in Biblical prophecy.

> The locusts were not allowed to kill them, only to inflict pain on them for five months; and the pain they caused was like the pain of a scorpion sting. In those days people will seek death but will not find it; they will long to die, but death will elude them. Now these locusts looked like horses outfitted for battle. On their heads were what looked like crowns of gold, and their faces were like human faces. They had hair like women's hair, and their teeth were like those of lions. Their chests were like iron breastplates, and the sound their wings made was like the roar of many horses and chariots rushing into battle. They had tails like those of scorpions, with stings; and in their tails was their power to hurt people for five months. They had as king over them the angel of the Abyss, whose name in Hebrew is "Abaddon" and in our language, "Destroyer."[30]

This army will cause people to suffer without allowing them to die. Yochanan can hardly imagine the type of physical and mental torture man is able to inflict to man. Yet, he hasn't even seen or heard of the cruelty of the Inquisition and of the Holocaust, nor of the effects of nuclear and chemical weapons.

> The first woe has passed, but there are still two woes to come.[31]

29. Joe 2:20
30. Rev 9:5–11
31. Rev 9:12

Yochanan has not yet recovered emotionally from the distresses of the first woe, when he immediately witnesses the events that constitute the sixth shofar, the second woe decreed upon mankind. "What kind of doom will the voice of the sixth shofar bring?" he wonders.

The Voice of the Sixth Shofar

> The sixth angel sounded his shofar, and I heard a voice from the four horns of the gold altar before God...[32]

Yochanan sees all these things from the vantage point of the Temple court, the place of the altar where he saw the souls of those who died for the name of Yeshua; the place where he heard their supplications for vindication. He sees inside what seems to be the first chamber of the Tabernacle. He sees the golden altar of incense where the prayers of Israel are brought before HaShem.

> Saying to the sixth angel, the one with the shofar, "Release the four angels that are bound at the great river Euphrates!" And they were released. These four angels had been kept ready for this moment, for this day and month and year, to kill a third of mankind.[33]

This speaks of a day, month, and year when four "angels" are destined to come out of the Euphrates River to kill a third of mankind. Yochanan realizes that whereas the voice of the fifth shofar brought suffering, the voice of the sixth brings death:

> And the number of cavalry soldiers was two hundred million! — I heard the number. Here are how the horses looked in the vision: the riders had breastplates that were fire-red, iris-blue and sulfur-yellow; the horses' heads were like lions' heads; and from their mouths issued fire, smoke and sulfur. It was these three plagues that killed a third of mankind — the fire, smoke and sulfur issuing from the horses' mouths. For the power of the horses was in their mouths — and also in their tails, for their tails were like snakes with heads, and with them they could cause injury.[34]

32. Rev 9:13
33. Rev 9:14–15
34. Rev 9:16–19

Yochanan sees soldiers come out of the abyss of the Euphrates. He knows this River as one that flowed in Eden. He sees a large army such as was never seen before. An army prepared for battle and for war. The black horse of the second seal comes to his mind! Israel, Yochanan's country, has been the battleground of so many wars. Yochanan knows that weapons do not have a heart or a soul that can discriminate between the guilty and the innocent. For a man of peace and love, this type of war for control over man's soul and destiny is where the degradation of mankind goes to its lowest point. It is the unraveling of a society that has repeatedly refused to live by HaShem's commandments.

> The rest of mankind, those who were not killed by these plagues, even then did not turn from what they had made with their own hands — they did not stop worshipping demons and idols made of gold, silver, bronze, stone and wood, which cannot see or hear or walk. Nor did they turn from their murdering, their involvement with the occult and with drugs, their sexual immorality or their stealing.[35]

Yochanan visualizes the times preceding the return of Mashiach. He sees that in spite of millennia of warnings through daily Torah admonitions by priests, rabbis, teachers, and emissaries; that in spite of his dreadful warnings and punishing discipline his people who should know better will continue to serve the works of their own hands instead of serving him. They will desire to work for meat which perishes and serve the Mammon of the rusting wealth of this world which cannot see, hear, speak, or walk. They will change the game rules and call "good," "evil," and "evil," "good,"[36] and in so doing justify their slaughtering of the innocent, their demonism, drugs, immorality, and theft.

Yochanan sadly remembers the words of his beloved friend and companion, Kefa, the one who died, crucified upside down at the pleasure of the Roman Emperor,

35. Rev 9:20–21
36. Isa 5:20

> For the time has come for the judgment to begin. It begins with the household of God; and if it starts with us [the emissaries], what will the outcome be for those who are disobeying God's Good News?[37]

In the days of the golden calf, Moshe stood as a mediator and intercessor between HaShem and Israel. In the days of Korach's rebellion, Aaron, following in the footsteps of his brother and mentor, also stood between HaShem and Israel. In days of the Kingdom, HaShem heard Amos' prayers for the people, as well as those of the High-Priest in the days of Joel and relented from the evil he had decreed on his people. Yochanan now wonders, "Is there one who will in these awful days be a mediator, an intercessor to stand between the congregations and HaShem's wrath?"

Yes! He remembers his own rabbi and Master, he who is a "cohen, priest, forever"; And even more, he knows, "how much better is the covenant of which Yeshua has become…a guarantor, because he lives forever, consequently, he is totally able to deliver those who approach God through him; since he is alive forever and thus forever able to intercede on their behalf."[38]

Yochanan understands that "atoned for" does not necessarily mean "unpunished," and that he who is truly repentant desires to do acts of repentance as restitution for his evil deeds. The trials and tribulations that purify the bride, the congregation of Messiah, have certainly come, first to the emissaries, then to the congregation of believers.[39]

Yochanan lifts his head to the gloomy screech of the vulture. His macabre circular dance presents an omen of more destruction. What will the voice of the seventh shofar, the third woe, bring upon humankind?

The Master Introduces the Seventh Shofar

> Next I saw another mighty angel coming down from heaven. He was dressed in a cloud, with a rainbow over his head; his face was like the sun, his legs like columns of fire.[40]

37. 1 Peter 4:17
38. Heb 7:21–25
39. 1 Peter 1:17
40. Rev 10:1

The Master, himself in his heavenly glory, comes to announce the seventh shofar: the third woe to befall humanity. Yochanan recognizes him because of his legs and his cloudy garment.[41] He also notices the majestic symbol of the rainbow, which he previously saw around the throne of the Ancient of Days.[42]

> And he had a little scroll lying open in his hand. He planted his right foot on the sea and his left foot on the land.[43]

As he stands on both land and sea, Mashiach shows that the next message is going to be universal.

> And shouted in a voice as loud as the roar of a lion; and when he shouted, seven thunderclaps sounded with voices that spoke…[44]

The Lion of Judah roars. He roars the words of the Almighty with all the divine power and authority given him. As in previous instances, his voice is accompanied by thunder.

> When the seven thunders spoke, I was about to write; but I heard a voice from heaven say, "Seal up the things the seven thunders said, do not write them down!"[45]

Now Yochanan joins the rank of the prophets, like Daniel who heard secrets "not to be revealed." Yochanan remembers Moshe's admonition to Israel, "Things which are hidden belong to ADONAI our God. But the things that have been revealed belong to us and our children forever, so that we can observe all the words of this Torah."[46]

> Then the angel I saw standing on the sea and on the land lifted his right hand toward heaven and swore by the One who lives forever and ever, who created heaven and what is in it, earth and what is in it, and the sea and what is in it.[47]

41. Rev 1:14–15
42. Rev 4:3
43. Rev 10:2
44. Rev 10:3
45. Rev 10:4
46. Deuteronomy 29:29
47. Rev 10:5–6

Yochanan can't help but remember his Master, who, alongside his other teachers, often admonished him about the dangers of swearing falsely by HaShem, by his throne, or even by the Temple. The Master must be pretty sure about what he is going to say:

> There will be no more delay; on the contrary, in the days of the sound from the seventh angel when he sounds his shofar, the hidden plan of God will be brought to completion.[48]

Yochanan hears it clearly. At the voice of the seventh shofar, the hidden plan, the mystery of the Good News, of the *Besorah* announced at Mount Horeb and by all the prophets, will be brought to completion. Yochanan knows about that hidden plan. Paul the emissary spoke of it. In a letter to the Roman congregation, he said:

> Now to God, who can strengthen you, according to my Good News, in harmony with the revelation of the secret truth which is the proclamation of Yeshua the Messiah, kept hidden in silence for ages and ages.[49]

He also speaks of it to the congregation in Corinth:

> Look, I will tell you a secret — not all of us will die! But we will all be changed! It will take but a moment, the blink of an eye, at the final shofar. For the shofar will sound, and the dead will be raised to live forever, and we too will be changed. For this material which can decay must be clothed with imperishability, this which is mortal must be clothed with immortality. When what decays puts on imperishability and what is mortal puts on immortality, then this passage in the Tanakh will be fulfilled: "Death is swallowed up in victory.[50]

The "mystery" he is talking about is the long-awaited final resurrection! After all this doom and gloom, finally, the greatly anticipated promise made by the sages of Israel and reinforced by his Master: The Final Resurrection. The ancient texts he studied in yeshiva rushed to his mind:

48. Rev 10:7
49. Rom 16:25
50. 1Co 15:51–54

> Our God is coming and not staying silent. With a fire devouring ahead of him and a great storm raging around him, he calls to the heavens above and to earth, in order to judge his people. "Gather to me my faithful, those who made a covenant with me by sacrifice." The heavens proclaim his righteousness, for God himself is judge.[51]

Also:

> Your dead will live, my corpse will rise; awake and sing, you who dwell in the dust; for your dew is like the morning dew, and the earth will bring the ghosts to life. Come, my people, enter your rooms, and shut your doors behind you. Hide yourselves for a little while until the wrath is past.[52]

As well as:

> When that time comes, Mikha'el, the great prince who champions your people, will stand up; and there will be a time of distress unparalleled between the time they became a nation and that moment. At that time, your people will be delivered, everyone whose name is found written in the book. Many of those sleeping in the dust of the earth will awaken, some to everlasting life and some to everlasting shame and abhorrence.[53]

This is:

> The Good News as he proclaimed it to his servants the prophets.[54]

Yochanan was familiar with this Good News as proclaimed by HaShem's servants, the prophets. He remembered telling the people of Israel about it, alongside his former teacher, Yochanan the Immerser. Oh, how the people approached them at the river with joy and gladness when they heard the message, Repent, the Kingdom of Heaven is at hand. They knew then that freedom from Rome's heavy-handed subjugation was coming soon. Israel was about to again become

51. Selah Ps 50:3–6
52. Isa 26:19–20
53. Dan 12:1–2
54. Rev 10:7

an independent sovereign nation with HaShem, ruling the world from Jerusalem through the agency of his Anointed Messiah King. Yochanan remembers when his own Master sent him with the other disciples to proclaim that very same message to all the cities of Israel. It was at the time a difficult message to believe, but it was not a new one. It was the manifest destiny of Israel as defined by the prophets and the sages of Israel.

When the Master died on the tree, all hope seemed to vanish. But how quickly did the newly born Messianic movement spread by leaps and bounds when he resurrected and showed himself to the people. Thousands of people rapidly joined the growing movement. So popular were they that even the Sadducee priests were afraid to touch them.[55] A few years later, the whole city of Jerusalem was full of believers who continued in Torah observance.[56]

A few decades after that, Yochanan saw his Israeli brothers turn against the movement. Later, he also witnessed the destruction of the Temple. The Roman Emperor ordered his death by boiling him in a cauldron of oil, but Yochanan wouldn't boil, so along with others from the Messianic community, he was exiled to the Isle of Patmos. Had it all been in vain? Was there still hope?

Yes! There was hope! Through the divine vision, Yochanan understands that there is much more work to be done. There will be a resurrection of the dead. The mysterious hidden plan will come to fruition and, in time, the message of the Good News will be fulfilled. Mashiach will come to reign over the earth in Jerusalem! We just need to wait for that seventh shofar: that third woe!

Yochanan Eats the Scroll!

> Next the voice which I had heard from heaven spoke to me again and said, "Go, take the scroll lying open in the hand of the angel standing on the sea and on the land!"[57]

55. Acts 4:21
56. Acts 21:20
57. Rev 10:8

> So I went over to the angel and asked him to give me the little scroll; and he said to me, "Take it and eat it. It will turn your stomach bitter, but in your mouth it will be sweet as honey."[58]

Yochanan doesn't explain what was written in the scroll, but the Master in his angelic form warns him of its effects. Yochanan pictures now the prophets Jeremiah and Ezekiel who were also asked to ingest a scroll that brought sweetness to their belly. In the case of Yochanan, it also makes his stomach bitter. A bitter-sweet message like that delivered by Shim'on to Miriam:

> Now, ADONAI, according to your word, your servant is at peace as you let him go; for I have seen with my own eyes your yeshu`ah, which you prepared in the presence of all peoples—a light that will bring revelation to the Goyim and glory to your people Isra'el.... This child will cause many in Isra'el to fall and to rise, he will become a sign whom people will speak against; moreover, a sword will pierce your own heart too. All this will happen in order to reveal many people's inmost thoughts."[59]

Yochanan takes the scroll from the Master and eats it:

> I took the little scroll from the angel's hand and ate it; and in my mouth it was sweet as honey; but after I had swallowed it, my stomach turned bitter. Then I was told, "You must prophesy again about many peoples, nations, languages and kings."[60]

Yochanan knew then that he will eventually leave the island. He had to if he were to prophesy to people, nations, languages, and kings. HaShem's words bring joy, but they also bring bitterness. Both HaShem's sweet redemptive forgiving grace and his bitter truth of requited justice are needed for iniquity in the world to be purged. His just judgments are indeed a sign of his forgiving grace. As the vulture continues to circle the sky, Yochanan waits for the voice of the seventh

58. Rev 10:9
59. Lu 2:29–35
60. Rev 10:10–11

shofar with a mix of fear and joyful anticipation. What will it bring that will complete HaShem's "hidden plan"?

Vision of a Third Temple

> I was given a measuring rod like a stick and told, "Get up, and measure the Temple of God and the altar, and count how many people are worshipping there![61]

The second Temple, built after the return from Babylon and beautified by King Herod, had been burnt and razed to the ground by Roman General Titus a few decades before. Yochanan sees another Temple in Jerusalem. He remembers the midrash of the prince's three garments. The exiled disciple leaps for joy. This can only mean the actual renaissance of Jewish worship in what could only be a future Temple in Jerusalem. He remembers HaShem's promises through Moshe at Kadesh Barnea:

> At that point, ADONAI your God will reverse your exile and show you mercy; he will return and gather you from all the peoples to which ADONAI your God scattered you. If one of yours was scattered to the far end of the sky, ADONAI your God will gather you even from there; he will go there and get you. ADONAI your God will bring you back into the land your ancestors possessed, and you will possess it; he will make you prosper there, and you will become even more numerous than your ancestors.[62]

After all the terrible things he had seen happening to his country, to his brothers and sisters, to the believers, to the disciples of Yeshua the visions on the Isle of Patmos give Yochanan a fuller perspective. Though the outlook is bleak, though his Master is "concealed" from his people, this concealment does not hamper the fulfillment of his promises. Even in this present exile, Yochanan understands that though invisible to the sight, silent to the ears, and impalpable to the touch, his Master is — and will forever be, present and active among

61. Rev 11:1
62. Deut 30:3–5

his people. Unknown to them all, he would return them to their land and fulfill the very thing that they expect from him: the rebuilding of the Temple. He will also eventually bring peace to a Jewish-owned Jerusalem, the place from where he will one day reign over Israel and over the nations. The disciple's heart leaps for joy at the sight of a rebuilt Temple in the Holy City of Jerusalem.

Yochanan is instructed to measure the Temple, to spiritually evaluate and gauge the virtue found in it. He remembers Zechariah who saw an angel measure a future Jerusalem in order to preserve her.[63] He also remembers Jeremiah who saw HaShem measuring Jerusalem in the days of King Manasseh for judgment and destruction.[64] Which is it this time? Is this third Temple measured for redemption, or for judgment?

The Temple is functional and active in the days of Jeremiah, but idolatry had infiltrated it and made it spiritually wanting. Yochanan could remember his Master taking a "measure" of the Temple while speaking against the hypocrisy found in it. Less than a century later, his disciples and the Jewish believers still in Jerusalem would see how radical fundamentalism, zealotry, and the causeless hatred of brother against brother would cause its destruction and the downfall of Jerusalem.

Yochanan is told to count the number of worshippers in the Temple. He is not told why. Yochanan understands that before redemption becomes personal, it is bestowed through a remnant or first fruit. Maybe, like in the case of S'dom in the days of Avraham, and of Shomron in the days of Eliyahu, this measuring and counting has to do with identifying a redeemed remnant. He could foresee that just like when they came out of Egypt and Babylon, an Israel returning from decades and centuries of exile would not necessarily be pure and Torah observant. She would need cleansing from her worldly idolatrous ways, as well as a righteous remnant to intercede for her.

63. Zech 2

64. 2 Kings 21:13; Lam 2:8

> But the court outside the Temple, leave that out; don't measure it; because it has been given to the Goyim, and they will trample over the holy city for forty-two months.[65]

This third Temple will be different from the first two. Its outer court will belong to the Gentiles. All Israel would control is the Tabernacle part made of its two main chambers: The Holy and the Holy of Holies. "It is not what it was before, but it is progress...," Yochanan thinks. At that time, it seems that Gentiles still inhabit and even control part of the Holy City of Jerusalem. "Will Jerusalem ever be fully sovereign again?" He often ponders these words of the sages who said that, "The Son of David will not come until even the pettiest kingdom stops having power over Israel, for it is written, 'He will cut off the shoots with pruning hooks, and he will hew down and remove the branches.'"[66] While Israelites will live and worship in Jerusalem at that time, the Gentiles will keep a certain part of it for forty-two months, or three and half years. Yochanan thinks of that period as the second half of the last 7 years before the returning of Messiah in Daniel's prophecy, a time of great persecution:

> He [the prince that is to come] will make a strong covenant with leaders for one week [of years]. For half of the week he will put a stop to the sacrifice and the grain offering. On the wing of detestable things the desolator will come and continue until the already decreed destruction is poured out on the desolator.[67]

Yochanan knows that these three and half years preceding the final establishment of the Messianic Age on earth are terrible:

> He [the Sheker Mashiach] will speak words against the Most High and try to exhaust the holy ones of the Most High. He will attempt to alter the seasons and the law; and [the holy ones] will be handed over to him for a time, times and half a time.[68]

65. Rev 11:2
66. Sanhedrin 98a
67. Dan 9:27
68. Dan 7:25

Two Witnesses

> Also I will give power to my two witnesses; and they will prophesy for 1,260 days, dressed in sackcloth.[69]

Yochanan is aware that Eliyahu the prophet precedes the arrival of Mashiach, but who is that second one? The disciple is not told the names of these two; he is only given their functions.

> These are the two olive trees and the two menorahs standing before the Lord of the earth.[70]

Yochanan knows about the two olive trees. In the days of Zechariah, they were Y'hoshua the Cohen HaGadol, and Z'rubavel, the governor. As religious and civil leaders working together, they represented the idea of "Priest and King," the perfect fullness of the government of the nation of Israel. These two were leaders of the returned exiles and of the rebuilding of the Temple following the Babylonian captivity. At a certain point, the building of the House of God was challenged by jealous enemies, but the prophets Haggai and Zechariah came to encourage these two leaders to lead the people into resuming the work. Zechariah gave one instruction to Governor Z'rubavel: "Not by force, and not by power, but by my Spirit," says ADONAI-Tzva'ot. The rebuilding of Israel and its Temple would not be won by the force of arms but by virtue of the Spirit of HaShem.

Would this Temple in the vision, without an outer court, be a future unfinished Temple? Will there be in those future days people, enemies of Israel, who will oppose its completion? Will two Israeli leaders, one civil and one religious, arise to challenge these enemy forces? Will these leaders in modern Israel be a light and strength and encouragement to the faithful of the Land? Or, could this refer to the returning Messiah as both Priest and King as he appeared in the vision?[71] Yochanan knows that the main messianic ministry of the Master is the reestablishing of the Temple:

---

69. Rev 11:3
70. Rev 11:4
71. see Rev 1

> My servant David will be king over them, and all of them will have one shepherd; they will live by my rulings and keep and observe my regulations. They will live in the land I gave to Ya`akov my servant, where your ancestors lived; they will live there — they, their children, and their grandchildren, forever; and David my servant will be their leader forever. I will make a covenant of peace with them, an everlasting covenant. I will give to them, increase their numbers, and set my sanctuary among them forever. My home will be with them; I will be their God, and they will be my people.[72]

In Zechariah's vision, the two witnesses are compared to two olive trees providing oil for the Temple menorah, which stands in front of the Holy of Holies. But in Yochanan's vision, the anointed ones pour oil into two menorahs.

> If anyone tries to do them harm, fire comes out of their mouth and consumes their enemies… (Rev 11:5)

Yochanan had seen many people claiming to be prophets.[73] They usually drew crowds of curious folks by claiming they had a new revelation of some sort. While impressing people with miracles of healing, they offered messages of doom and destruction that usually ended up being as the Master's brother described, ."..waterless clouds carried along by the winds; trees without fruit even in autumn."[74] But these two witnesses had not only the words; they had the actions to match the words:

> Yes, if anyone tries to harm them, that is how he must die. They have the authority to shut up the sky, so that no rain falls during the period of their prophesying; also they have the authority to turn the waters into blood and to strike the earth with every kind of plague as often as they want.[75]

Here, Yochanan's curiosity gets the better of him. "Is it Eliyahu who shut up the sky as he tried to turn the Northern Kingdom away from

72. Ezek 37:24–27
73. Mt 24:11
74. Jude 12
75. Rev 11:5–6

idolatry?" After all, he is known to have never died and he is supposed to return! Is it Moshe who turned water into blood and called plagues on the earth against Egypt's Pharaoh? There was no witness to Moshe's death, so he has often been considered. Could it be Enoch, the prophet who challenged the Nephilim in the days of Noah and who is also known to have never died? Both Moshe and Eliyahu appeared alongside Yeshua on the Mount of Transfiguration. The disciples saw and heard them testify to the Master's mission. They saw Moshe as a representative of the Torah, and Eliyahu, a representative of the times of the prophets. Together, they showed the disciples that both the Books of the Torah and the Books of the Prophets bear witness of the Master.[76] One thing was sure; Eliyahu had to be one of those two prophets in the vision. Just as the Master taught his disciples, a second century midrash teaches about two comings of Eliyahu.[77] After all, if the Master comes twice, Eliyahu also needs to come twice. Both may have come the first time in weakness, but as we can see, they will come in power the second time. In any case, Yochanan sees the repetition of history.

> When they finish their witnessing, the beast coming up out of the Abyss will fight against them, overcome them and kill them.[78]

Yochanan knows that his teachers often used the imagery of "the abyss" or "the bottom of the sea" to talk about the kingdom of darkness. He wonders, "This beast; a similitude to evil Pharaoh as the Sea Monster of Egypt, spoken by both Isaiah and Ezekiel?[79] Will it revive? Will there be a devil-inspired powerful leader like Pharaoh who will again try to destroy Israel by silencing her prophets?"

> And their dead bodies will lie in the main street of the great city whose name, to reflect its spiritual condition, is "S'dom" and "Egypt" — the city where their Lord was executed on a stake.[80]

76. John 5:39
77. Mt 17:11-12; Seder Olam Rabbah
78. Rev 11:7
79. Isa: 51:9; Ezek:29:3
80. Rev 11:8

Yochanan is broken-hearted. The dragon succeeded in killing the leaders of Israel in Jerusalem itself. He must have remembered what his Master said,

> Yerushalayim! Yerushalayim! You kill the prophets! You stone those who are sent to you! How often I wanted to gather your children, just as a hen gathers her chickens under her wings, but you refused! Look! God is abandoning your house to you, leaving it desolate. For I tell you, from now on, you will not see me again until you say, "Blessed is he who comes in the name of ADONAI."[81]

> Some from the nations, tribes, languages and peoples see their bodies for three-and-a-half days and do not permit the corpses to be placed in a tomb. The people living in the Land rejoice over them, they celebrate and send each other gifts, because these two prophets tormented them so.[82]

Yochanan sees people worshipping in the Temple,[83] but outside, in the outer court, the people of the nations rejoiced. He sees them rejoicing at the cruel death of these leaders who challenged their godlessness. The impious rage of the Idumeans who helped the Roman conquer of Jerusalem is still fresh in the old apostle's mind. How can he not remember? Both the prophet Y'hoshua, and his father Ananias tried to warn the people in their days. They both stood as prophets in the midst of a doomed Jerusalem, warning of an imminent Roman invasion. The Idumeans were not happy to just kill all the people, but they cruelly murdered these two prophets and cast them out without burial, thus exposing their bodies to shame, corruption, and to the rapacious animals rampaging in the city. Now, Yochanan sees this sad page of Israel's history as an omen of things to come.

> But after the three-and-a-half days, a breath of life from God entered them, they stood up on their feet, and great fear fell on those who saw them.[84]

81. Mat 23:37–39
82. Rev 11:9–10
83. Rev 11:1
84. Rev 11:11

To Yochanan's surprise, the scenario is different this time. There will not be a repeat after all. Like with Lazarus, even after the body of the two prophets started decomposing, they are raised from the dead. Now he sees a different future. He envisions HaShem laughing at their futile efforts and sending to them the one to whom they will have to bend the knee in allegiance: Messiah, the conquering ruler of the earth. With all his heart, Yochanan now proclaims with King David:

> Why are the nations in an uproar, the peoples grumbling in vain? The earth's kings are taking positions, leaders conspiring together, against ADONAI and his anointed. They cry, "Let's break their fetters! Let's throw off their chains!" He who sits in heaven laughs; ADONAI looks at them in derision. Then in his anger he rebukes them, terrifies them in his fury. "I myself have installed my king on Tziyon, my holy mountain." "I will proclaim the decree: ADONAI said to me, 'You are my son; today I became your father. Ask of me, and I will make the nations your inheritance; the whole wide world will be your possession. You will break them with an iron rod, shatter them like a clay pot.' Therefore, kings, be wise; be warned, you judges of the earth. Serve ADONAI with fear; rejoice, but with trembling. Kiss the son lest he be angry, and you perish along the way, when suddenly his anger blazes. How blessed are all who take refuge in him.[85]

> Then the two heard a loud voice from heaven saying to them, "Come up here!" And they went up into heaven in a cloud, while their enemies watched them.[86]

As if it isn't enough, Yochanan sees these witnesses summoned by a heavenly voice. This voice reiterated the very words that he heard when he was asked to come up to HaShem's throne room, Come up here!

It is with great awe and excitement that Yochanan watches the two witnesses ascend from the earth in a cloud. It reminds him of the way the Master ascended in the clouds. Some believed in those days that so did Moshe.[87]

---

85. Ps 2:1–12
86. Rev11:12
87. Acts 1:9; Josephus, Antiquities of the Jews 4:8:48

The Earthquake

> In that hour there was a great earthquake, and a tenth of the city collapsed. Seven thousand people were killed in the earthquake, and the rest were awestruck and gave glory to the God of heaven.[88]

This is the great moment he has been waiting for. The moment Paul expected when he said, "and that it is in this way that all Isra'el will be saved. As the Tanakh says, "Out of Tziyon will come the Redeemer; he will turn away ungodliness from Ya`akov."[89] The moment Yeshua spoke of: "For I tell you, from now on, you will not see me again until you say, "Blessed is he who comes in the name of ADONAI."[90] It is the moment all the prophets from the beginning of time saw and hoped for; the moment of the full redemption of Israel. The words of the ancient prophet race through his mind as he watches the Jerusalem earthquake:

> On that day, his feet will stand on the Mount of Olives, which lies to the east of Yerushalayim; and the Mount of Olives will be split in half from east to west, to make a huge valley. Half of the mountain will move toward the north, and half of it toward the south. You will flee to the valley in the mountains, for the valley in the mountains will reach to Atzel. You will flee, just as you fled before the earthquake in the days of `Uziyah king of Y'hudah. Then ADONAI my God will come to you with all the holy ones. On that day, there will be neither bright light nor thick darkness; and one day, known to ADONAI, will be neither day nor night, although by evening there will be light. On that day, fresh water will flow out from Yerushalayim, half toward the eastern sea and half toward the western sea, both summer and winter. Then ADONAI will be king over the whole world. On that day ADONAI will be the only one, and his name will be the only name.[91]

The Jerusalem earthquake causes much anguish and pain. Like most of us, Yochanan had to deal with much pain, physical, spiritual, or emotional pain. He remembered the words of his colleague to the Corinthian congregation:

---

88. Rev 11:13
89. Rom 11:26
90. Mt 23:39
91. Zech 14:4–9

> Pain handled in God's way produces a turning from sin to God which leads to salvation, and there is nothing to regret in that![92]

The pain produced by the earthquake, by the partial destruction of Jerusalem, and by the grieving over the dead, provokes needed repentance. As a result, the rest were awestruck and gave glory to the God of heaven. Jewish sages always proclaimed that only the repentance of the Jewish people will bring Messiah.

The second woe has passed.[93]

The vulture ominously continues his macabre circular dance in the sky.

The Voice of the Seventh Shofar

> See, the third woe is coming quickly. The seventh angel sounded his shofar.[94]

Yochanan suddenly remembered the proclamation concerning the seventh shofar:

> In the days of the sound from the seventh angel when he sounds his shofar, the hidden plan of God will be brought to completion, the Good News as he proclaimed it to his servants the prophets.[95]

> And there were loud voices in heaven, saying, "The kingdom of the world has become the Kingdom of our Lord and his Messiah, and he will rule forever and ever!"[96]

The time when the seventh shofar blows is a defining moment. It is the time when Messiah comes to reign. It is the time when the Messianic Age is finally fulfilled; when the Kingdom of God is established on earth as it is in heaven, with Mashiach ruling over the world from Jerusalem. At the time of the blowing of his seventh shofar, Yochanan sees:

> The twenty-four elders sitting on their thrones in God's presence fell on their faces and worshipped God, saying, "We thank you,

---

92. 2 Co 7:10
93. (Rev 11:14)
94. (Rev 11:14–15)
95. Rev 10:7
96. Rev 11:15

> ADONAI, God of heaven's armies, the One who is and was, that you have taken your power and have begun to rule.[97]

As if needing to find scriptural documentation for their praise, Yochanan hears the elders quote and paraphrase David's famous psalm:

> The Goyim raged. But now your rage has come, the time for the dead to be judged, the time for rewarding your servants the prophets and your holy people, those who stand in awe of your name, both small and great. It is also the time for destroying those who destroy the earth.[98]

To his great awe, Yochanan witnesses the climax of the fall feasts.

The Temple opens to display the Ark

> Then the Temple of God in heaven was opened.[99]
>
> And the Ark of the Covenant was seen in his Temple; and there were flashes of lightning, voices, peals of thunder, an earthquake and violent hail.[100]

Yochanan beholds the ark. Not the one carved with hands, which Jeremiah hid in a cave by Mount Nebo before the conquest of Jerusalem. Not one of the copies that were made. In front of him lies the original Ark from heaven. The one Moshe saw when he was on the Mount. Yochanan felt so honored! He knew that in the days of the Exodus from Egypt, the presence of the Ark signaled HaShem's presence guiding his people. In the same manner, in those terrible days to come, the appearance of the heavenly Ark assures him of the presence of the Ancient of Days again about to fulfill the rest of his covenanted promises. As the vulture continues its death dance in the sky, Yochanan remembers.

---

97. Rev 11:16–17
98. Rev 11:18
99. Rev 11:19
100. Rev 11:19

Miriam in the Sky with the Dragon/Tanin

> Now a great sign was seen in heaven, a woman clothed with the sun, under her feet the moon, and on her head a crown of twelve stars.[101]

Yochanan remembers the Master's words that echoed those of the prophets, "There will appear signs in the sun, moon and stars; and on earth."[102] He was used to looking at the stars of the middle-eastern night skies. He pondered on the astronomical events that gave the signal to the Persian magis that the long-prophesied king of Israel was born. Until this day, Yochanan never closes the Shabbat without seeking for the three first stars that illuminate the evening sky to announce havdalah, the beginning of the new week. He could find his way in these astral bodies. He can recognize the times and seasons of Shabbats and festivals just by looking at the constellations.

He remembers that fall festival season when some time before his Master's birth the, "woman clothed with the sun, under her feet the moon, and on her head a crown of twelve stars…" was seen in the heavens. Later, he hears about the testimony of the magis who read the signs in the skies through the movement of Jupiter and Regulus through Arieh and Betula, to know when they should come and worship the King of Israel.

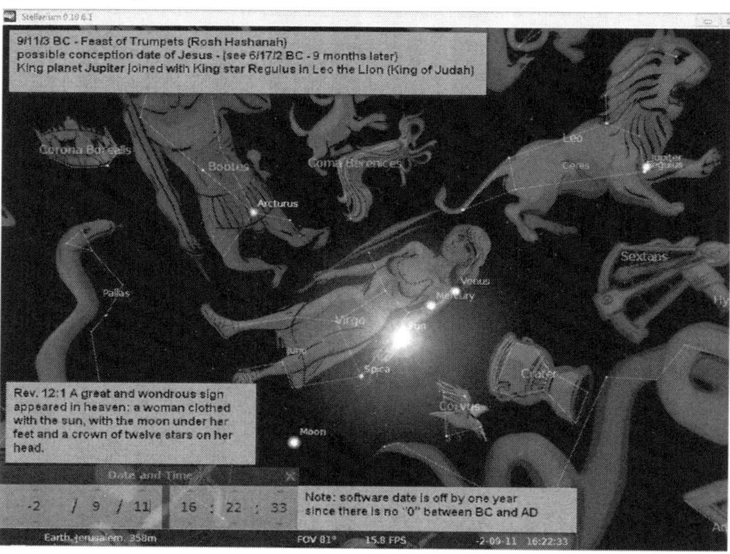

101. Rev 12:1
102. Luke 21:25

Yochanan often quoted King David:

> The heavens declare the glory of God, the dome of the sky speaks the work of his hands. Every day it utters speech, every night it reveals knowledge. Without speech, without a word, without their voices being heard,[103]

Yochanan keeps looking to the sky and remembers:

> She was pregnant and about to give birth, and she screamed in the agony of labor. (Rev 12:2)

How beautiful it was to see Jupiter, the king planet, and Regulus the king star move from Arieh (Leo constellation) to Betula (Virgo constellation), as if coming out of her womb. The heavens truly declared HaShem's glory at the time the king from the Lion of the tribe of Judah was born.[104]

> Another sign was seen in heaven: there was a great red dragon with seven heads and ten horns, and on its heads were seven royal crowns. Its tail swept a third of the stars out of heaven and threw them down to the earth. It stood in front of the woman about to give birth, so that it might devour the child the moment it was born. (Rev 12:3–4)

At that time, he hadn't noticed the Tanin serpent residing near Betula, as if waiting to devour her offspring. The message of the constellations was clear to Yochanan. The old shaliach did not need the stars to tell him of Israel's history, which raced through his mind. Hadn't it always been so?

From its very inception at the birth of Abraham, the nation's destiny has been threatened with annihilation, a threat which has repeated itself throughout the ages, and the days of Yeshua are no exception. Yochanan knows of wicked King Nimrod the descendant of Ham, the son of Noah. Nimrod was once told by his magicians about a certain new star that had risen in the east. His astrologers warned him that this new star heralded the birth of a challenger from the tribe of Shem. In

103. (Ps 19:1–3)
104. Ps 19 :1–6

his insecurity, Nimrod, who was so fearful, asked for all newborns to be killed.

The vision became in Yochanan a crucible for all the women of Israel who suffered or fought to preserve the precious seed. Most of all, the woman in the vision reminded Yochanan of Miriam, the mother of the Master, but also of Abraham's mother who feared for her son. Yochebed,the mother of Moshe, also came to his mind when he thought of Miriam chosen to protect the Light and Glory of Israel from King Herod and his soldiers. With the twelve stars around her head and as a descendant of the Davidic kingly tribe, the woman in the vision is portrayed as a royal representative of the twelve tribes of Israel, a symbolic image of HaShem's bride.[105] She (Israel) would give birth to him who will return the children back to their Father, bringing with them all the nations of the world to the covenant of Israel.

In this time-transcending vision, the Tanin (the serpent who from the beginning of time had been in opposition to HaShem's plans) is back to his old tricks. As always, he is scheming for the annihilation of Israel, and this time, of Messianic Israel right from its very conception. The old disciple discerns the cosmic evil behind all those past, present, and future, who have tried, who try and will try to extinguish the light of Israel.

The imagery stimulates Yochanan's mind. From Egypt to Assyria, followed by Babylon, Medo-Persia, Greece, and now Rome, seeing with the imagery of Daniel's vision, everything is clear. It seemed that this evil dragon is the cosmic power and inspiration behind each of these seven major dominant powers in the world, those powers that tried to annihilate Israel. "But why?" he wonders. "We're so small! What threat could we represent? Does it really take a world-class power to get rid of us?"

Yochanan notices that this Tanin has seven heads, not six. "Will there be another major world power who will try to annihilate Israel?" he wonders. Will it succeed? And if not, at what price? As Yochanan pondered the vision, the vulture continues circling the skies. He remembered the angels who fell from their heavenly state in the days of the prophet Noah. He and Kefa studied it together in the writings

105. Ezek 16:1-14

of pre-Flood prophet and first-ever scribe: Enoch. Kefa was great at teaching about these things. He had noticed that some believers tended to think that HaShem's mercy excluded the need for retribution for sin. In order to balance their understanding of HaShem's mercy and compassion with truth, in one of his letters, Kefa made a midrash as he reminded them of the punished angels.

> For God did not spare the angels who sinned; on the contrary, he put them in gloomy dungeons lower than Sh'ol to be held for judgment.[106]

Miriam's offspring was of prime importance: he who would finally fulfill Abraham's prophecies and bring about Israel's final destiny. No wonder the Tanin stood there waiting for him to emerge.

She gave birth to a son, a male child, the one who will rule all the nations with a staff of iron. (Rev 12:5)

Isaiah's words to King Ahab[107]rush through his mind[108]. The prophetic oracle about the woman's male offspring who will rule all the nations reminds Yochanan of the stories that circulated in Jerusalem at the time of the earthly birth of his Master. Having spent nearly three years with Yeshua, he can now make sense of the precious words of Simeon when Miriam and Yoseph brought their new baby boy Yeshua for the *Pidyon-haben* פדיון הבן (redemption of the firstborn at the time of her purification.[109] According to his own testimony, Simeon had gone to the Temple's courts that day, following the leading of HaShem's Spirit. When he saw Yoseph, Miriam, and their baby, Yeshua, Simeon said that at that moment, he was taken by an irresistible urge, he

> Took him in his arms, made a b'rakhah to God, and said, "Now, ADONAI, according to your word, your servant is at peace as you let him go; for I have seen with my own eyes your yeshu`ah [Hebrew for: salvation], which you prepared in the presence of all

106. 2 Peter 2:4
107. Is 7:14
108. Mt 1:23
109. Lev 12:1–8

> peoples—a light that will bring revelation to the Goyim and glory to your people Isra'el."[110]

At that moment, Simeon saw that:

> Yeshua's father and mother were marveling at the things Shim`on was saying about him.[111]

And to their big surprise:

> Shim`on blessed them and said to the child's mother, Miriam,
>
> "This child will cause many in Isra'el to fall and to rise, he will become a sign whom people will speak against; moreover, a sword will pierce your own heart too. All this will happen in order to reveal many people's inmost thoughts."[112]

Yoseph and Miriam were still confounded by these words when another wonderful thing happened that day:

> There was also a prophet named Hannah Bat-P'nu'el, of the tribe of Asher. She was a very old woman — she had lived with her husband seven years after her marriage and had remained a widow ever since; now she was eighty-four. She never left the Temple grounds but worshipped there night and day, fasting and praying. She came by at that moment and began thanking God and speaking about the child to everyone who was waiting for Yerushalayim to be liberated.[113]

Bringing his racing thoughts back, Yochanan wants to know the rest of the oracle from Yeshua. He was not surprised.

Her child was snatched up to God and his throne.[114]

Yochanan knows that his Master had been taken up to sit at the right hand of HaShem's throne. The Master told him so,[115] and he saw him there in the throne room when he was invited to come up. The

110. Lu 2:28–32
111. Lu 2:33
112. Lu 2:34–35
113. Lu 2:36–38
114. Rev 12:5
115. Lu 22:69

disciple had also witnessed the day when Yeshua was snatched up to heaven in a cloud.[116]

> And she [the woman] fled into the desert, where she has a place prepared by God so that she can be taken care of for 1,260 days.[117]

These words reminded Yochanan of the times preceding the destruction of the Jerusalem Temple by General Titus. Yeshua had warned them of the evil days to come upon Jerusalem, which did not recognize her opportunity when HaShem offered it.

Up to the war years, the Jerusalem community had been the religious nerve of the Messianic movement, but everything changed in the war with Rome. As Yochanan heard of Sha'ul's beheading; of Kefa's and Andrew's crucifixion; of Timotheus' arrest; when news leaked of the death of Nero, of the civil wars that ensued, of the wars in Galilee and in Judea, of the persecution of the disciples by their own Jewish brothers, he couldn't help but remember these words of the Master which, like those of the prophet Jeremiah, while being rejected by an unbelieving nation, vindicated his prophetic gift as well as the disciples who followed him:

Peoples will fight each other, nations will fight each other.[118]

> They will arrest you and persecute you, handing you over to the synagogues and prisons; and you will be brought before kings and governors. This will all be on account of me, but it will prove an opportunity for you to bear witness. ... You will be betrayed even by parents, brothers, relatives and friends; some of you they will have put to death; and everyone will hate you because of me.[119]

To whichever sect of Judaism, they belonged, the fall of Jerusalem and the destruction of the Temple broke people's hearts. Oh, how the Master had warned them about it:

116. Acts 1:9
117. Rev 12:6
118. Lu 21:10
119. Lu 21:12–17

> However, when you see Yerushalayim surrounded by armies, then you are to understand that she is about to be destroyed. Those in Y'hudah must escape to the hills, those inside the city must get out, and those in the country must not enter it. For these are the days of vengeance when everything that has been written in the Tanakh will come true. What a terrible time it will be for pregnant women and nursing mothers! For there will be great distress in the Land and judgment on the people. Some will fall by the edge of the sword, others will be carried into all the countries of the Goyim, and Yerushalayim will be trampled down by the Goyim until the age of the Goyim has run its course.[120]

Those were the days after the martyrdom of Ya'akov HaTzaddik, the brother of Yeshua. Shim'on ben K'lofah was the elder of the Israeli congregations. Many believers had already fled to Pella upon the arrival of the Roman divisions. Many signs and wonders occurred in view of all the people in the city. The false prophets of the politics of denial interpreted these signs as positive omens, but those who kept the words of the Master, who prophesied a generation beforehand, rightfully understood them as the imminent destruction of Jerusalem. Yochanan especially remembered the reports that on a certain evening, just as the Master said would happen:

> Before sun-setting, chariots and troops of soldiers in their armor were seen running about among the clouds, and surrounding of cities.[121]

The disciples heeded the words of the Master and fled the city, rejoining those who had already gone. Yochanan sometimes cried as he heard reports of the horrible atrocities that befell the people of Jerusalem, as well as the Temple. At the same time, he is thankful for all the believers who obeyed the voice of the Master and fled. They had prayed for years for that day not falling on a Shabbat day or in the winter months, so that their traveling would not be impaired. They felt

120. Lu 21:20–24

121. Josephus, War of the Jews. Book 6; chapter 3, p296–299

that their prayers were answered, as this happened in the fall near the feast of Rosh Hashanah. Because of the words of the Master:

> There will appear signs in the sun, moon and stars; and on earth, nations will be in anxiety and bewilderment at the sound and surge of the sea, as people faint with fear at the prospect of what is overtaking the world; for the powers in heaven will be shaken. And then they will see the Son of Man coming in a cloud with tremendous power and glory. When these things start to happen, stand up and hold your heads high; because you are about to be liberated![122]

They spent their first Yom Kippur and Sukkot out of Jerusalem, waiting for a heavenly deliverance which did not come. It would be for another day.

The Pella community of believers decided to officially return to re-establish their community in Jerusalem in the fourth year after the destruction of the Temple.

Yochanan sees the vision of the "woman" fleeing to a place prepared for her for 1260 days, and he wonders, "Does this speak of our Pella exile?" Suddenly, he understands the great, cosmic plan. The community didn't die, but was reestablished on the slopes of Mt. Zion in Jerusalem. Together, they still meet in that room where they had the last seder with the Master, by King David's tomb. Finally, he understands what the prophet Isaiah spoke of:

> On that day, the remnant of Isra'el, those of the house of Ya`akov who escaped, will no longer rely on the man who struck them down, but will truly rely on ADONAI, the Holy One of Isra'el. A remnant will return, the remnant of Ya`akov, to the mighty God. For, although your people, Isra'el, are like the sand of the sea, only a remnant of them will return. Destruction is decreed, overflowing with justice. ADONAI Elohim-Tzva'ot will bring about this decreed destruction throughout all the land. Therefore ADONAI Elohim-Tzva'ot says: "My people living in Tziyon, don't be afraid of Ashur [Rome] even

122. Lu 21:25–28

> when he strikes you with a stick and raises his staff against you, the way it was in Egypt.[123]

A remnant remains to reach the whole world. Another spiritual veil is lifted and Yochanan is privy to the spiritual battles that go on behind these cosmic events.

> Next there was a battle in heaven — Mikha'el and his angels fought against the dragon, and the dragon and his angels fought back. But it was not strong enough to win, so that there was no longer any place for them in heaven. The great dragon was thrown out, that ancient serpent, also known as the Devil and Satan [the Adversary], the deceiver of the whole world. [124]

The Tanin has lost access to the heavenly realms. He and all the angels who pledged allegiance to him are refused all access to the divine presence. The Master had won the heavenly battle. HaSatan's power is defeated. He loses all power and authority in heaven, as it was given to Yeshua the Mashiach. Yochanan suddenly hears:

> He [the serpent] was hurled down to the earth, and his angels were hurled down with him[125]

Is this good news or bad news? Now, HaSatan and his minions are going to establish their headquarters on the earth. Yochanan worries for his brothers and sisters when he hears:

> A loud voice in heaven saying, "Now have come God's victory, power and kingship, and the authority of his Messiah; because the Accuser of our brothers, who accuses them day and night before God, has been thrown out![126]

The victory is won. He who constantly stood before HaShem bringing accusations against Israel will not be given audience anymore in front of the great Judge of the earth. Mikha'el and his angels won the battle.

123. Isa 10:20–24
124. Rev 12:7–9
125. Rev 12:9
126. Rev 12:10

Yochanan wonders, "Why was this victory won in heaven right when the offspring of the woman was snatched up? Did Master Yeshua have anything to do with it?" Oh, yes, he did! He, as the Blood Avenger, the Kinsman Redeemer, he who intercedes day and night, brought our prayers and tears to his Father. Mission accomplished. Yochanan remembered how from the beginning, HaSatan was trying to ensure the failure of Yeshua's mission. First, he inspired Herod to cut his life short. Then, at the beginning of his ministry, right after his immersion by Yochanan the Immerser, HaSatan met him in the desert after the Master had fasted for 40 days. The vile angel then tempted Yeshua to misuse the power of the Spirit of his Father. He suggested for him to use it for his own safety, comfort, and needs, such as changing a rock into bread, like a mere magician. HaSatan also tried to tell the Master to impress the masses by throwing himself from the pinnacle of the Jerusalem Temple. To remain alive, would certainly impress people as they witness a supernatural feat. They would certainly welcome him as a prophet then. HaSatan would even himself crowned Yeshua as king of the world, all for a simple genuflection. What was it HaSatan was afraid of? Yeshua did not respond to these attempts to satisfy the lust of the flesh, the lust of the eyes, and even the pride of life.[127] He knew about these old, evil tricks that had worked on Eve 4,000 years before.[128] Using the strength of his committed dedication to obey the Torah, Yeshua fought back HaSatan's advances, throwing at him all the power of the very words of his Father. Yochanan could also remember how HaSatan tempted the Master the night before execution, literally begging him to not go through with it. He didn't want Yeshua to die. He was offering him a way out. Was he afraid of Yeshua's work? It would certainly be the demise of his rule over death. But Yeshua had to die for the resurrection to take place.

> They defeated [Mikha'el and his angels] him because of the Lamb's blood and because of the message of their witness. Even when facing death, they did not cling to life.[129]

---

127. 1 John 2;16
128. Gen 3:6
129. Rev 12:11

Yochanan leaps for joy as he is given a glimpse at the end. Not only was the victory won by the faithfulness, work, and suffering of the Master, but also because of his own faithfulness and suffering, as well as that of his friends, brothers, and sisters. Exiled to the Isle, he sometimes got discouraged and even wondered if it had been the best decision to resist the Emperor's evil decree, but now he knows that everything will be okay. Those very words by the Master reassure him that his suffering, as well as that of his brothers and sisters, has not been in vain.

> Therefore, rejoice, heaven and you who live there! But woe to you, land and sea, for the Adversary has come down to you, and he is very angry, because he knows that his time is short![130]

Good news and bad news. Yes, the spiritual battle in the headquarters of heaven is won, but now it is time for hand-to-hand combat right here on earth. Yochanan understands why things had gotten worse since the Master's departure to his father's side. It was not as some believed, that HaShem had abandoned them, neither as some others proclaimed that they were lost in heretical teachings. But it was because victory was near. HaSatan knows it, so he throws everything he has at those he considers his enemies. But who are these enemies of HaSatan?

> When the dragon saw that he had been hurled down to the earth, he went in pursuit of the woman who had given birth to the male child.[131]

Yochanan watched the contemporary history of Israel being subjected to the angry fits of an unforgiving enemy, an enemy who took his revenge on HaShem's children, on his bride, on his people, on Israel. Yielding to Rome's temper and to their inability to give way to reason, just like in the days of Jeremiah when Israel provoked Babylon and was taken to captivity, Israel provoked Rome to the destruction of the Temple. It was all-out war. Being knowledgeable of prophecies and ancient midrashes, Yochanan could not be surprised at what would come next: total exile. He probably knew it from his studies that

130. (Rev 12:12)
131. (Rev 12:13)

just like Sarah, Abraham's wife was taken captive, twice, the city of Jerusalem would suffer two captivities. This will be the second one: the Roman exile.

> But the woman was given the two wings of the great vulture, so that she could fly to her place in the desert, where she is taken care of for a season and two seasons and half a season, away from the serpent's presence.[132]

Israel would be exiled in the Temple-less, Torah-less wilderness of the world. The desert is bad news, but it is also good news. It is in the wilderness that Israel meets her God. The prophet Ezekiel tells us all about it. As he spoke of Israel's espousals, of her defiant adulteries and disobediences, he also tells us about her final repentant return.[133]

> The serpent spewed water like a river out of its mouth after the woman, in order to sweep her away in the flood; but the land came to her rescue — it opened its mouth and swallowed up the river which the dragon had spewed out of its mouth.[134]

Yochanan watches the future of his people. He sees the dragon who, not unlike Pharaoh of old, tries to drown Israel; Israel who now inhabits the wilderness of the world and has found refuge in it through partial assimilation. Yochanan may have remembered Moshe's timeless warning to Israel concerning disobedience:

> I call on the sky and the earth to witness against you today that you will quickly disappear from the land that you are crossing the Yarden to possess. You will not prolong your days there but will be completely destroyed. ADONAI will scatter you among the peoples; and among the nations to which ADONAI will lead you away, you will be left few in number. There you will serve gods which are the product of human hands, made of wood and stone, which can't see, hear, eat or smell…

132. Rev 12:14
133. Ezek 16
134. Rev 12:15–16

Yochanan knows that the wilderness will bring Israel to her God.[135]

> The dragon was infuriated over the woman and went off to fight the rest of her children, those who obey God's commands and bear witness to Yeshua.[136]

Having failed to catch the offspring of the woman, and with its seed scattered in the nations of the world, the infuriated Tanin is now cast out of heaven, to the earth, where he will relentlessly pursue the seed of the offspring of the woman.

Could things become worse for followers of Yeshua? Could he imagine that the Messianic movement, of those who obey HaShem's commands and bear witness to Yeshua,[137] will one day be completely eradicated by the offspring of the very Gentiles the Jewish disciples sought to bring to the covenant of Israel? Maybe he did, but as usual, it is good news and bad news. Suffering and death followed by resurrection is the pattern. The vulture continues his sinister circular dance in the sky.

The Tanin, the Beast ... and the Other Beast

The infuriated Tanin now directs his choler towards the seed of the offspring of the woman. He continues his pursuit with uncontrollable rage and cruelty. Like an evil magician, he resorts to the lowest of all the incantations in his bag. He is determined to see to see the ultimate annihilation of his mortal final enemy: the seed of the woman, who obeys God's commands and bear witness to Yeshua.

> And I saw a beast come up out of the sea, with ten horns and seven head.[138]

The Tanin, now being refused access to the heavenly realms, establishes himself to work his plan through the governments of man on the earth. Yochanan heard of that sea monster. He read about it in the book of

135. Deut 4:26–31
136. Rev 12:1–17
137. Rev 12:17
138. Rev 13:1

creation. He remembers Job's great sea serpent, Ezekiel prophesying its demise; Moshe insulting Pharaoh's pride by contending he had control over those creatures of the Nile that Pharaoh sacrificed the Hebrew males to; and Isaiah prophesying of the eventual punishment on Leviathan and Rahab "who is Egypt."[139]

From the time he tempted Eve, used Cain to kill Abel, made attempts on Abraham, Moshe, and Yeshua's lives at birth and even opposed the matriarchs in bearing children, his fate was always within HaShem's control. Hosea the prophet saw HaShem use the beastly governments of the earth one after the other to discipline Israel, his firstborn. In spite of his doomed destiny, even in Yochanan's days, he persecutes and kills those who dare to follow HaShem. Doesn't he know? From the Garden of Eden his demise has always been certain. Why does he even try? Daniel the prophet saw each of the world Empires that persecuted Israel as monstrous evil beasts, each one eventually losing their power. Rome was the last beast of the prophecy, but the most terrible one. He remembers the words of the prophets:

> After this, I looked in the night visions; and there before me was a fourth animal, dreadful, horrible, extremely strong, and with great iron teeth. It devoured, crushed and stamped its feet on what was left. It was different from all the animals that had gone before it, and it had ten horns.[140]

Yochanan couldn't help but think of the ten horns on the head of this monster. Titus, the tenth Emperor over the Roman Empire, was the one who had the Holy Temple destroyed.

> On its horns were ten royal crowns and on its heads blasphemous names. The beast which I saw was like a leopard, but with feet like those of a bear and a mouth like the mouth of a lion.[141]

Rome seemed to be HaSatan's final and ultimate tool against the "Seed" of Eve. First, orchestrating Yeshua's crucifixion and then seeking to destroy his disciples. Yochanan remembers the prophecies

139. Is 30:7
140. Dan 7:7
141. Rev 13:1–2

he learned as a young Torah student. In this monstrous sea creature, he sees the Grecian leopard, the Assyrian bear, and the Roman lion of the visions of Daniel. This sea creature is very powerful but not of its own power:

> To it the dragon gave its power, its throne and great authority.[142]

Just as HaShem's name lived in Jerusalem with Israel as a representative of his Kingdom on earth, the Tanin lived in Rome, in and through the Roman Empire, as the representative of his earthly power. As the Tanin tried to swallow the Messiah child at birth through Herod, the Empire tried to kill Messiah at birth. As the Tanin pursued the seed of the woman, now the Roman Empire pursues and persecutes those who obey God's commands and bear witness to Yeshua. The Tanin gave all authority to his Empire on earth to do so. The battle which was formerly fought in the heavens has now come down to the realm of mankind. It is a battle to the finish but Yochanan knows the end already.

> One of the heads of the beast appeared to have received a fatal wound, but its fatal wound was healed, and the whole earth followed after the beast in amazement.[143]

In each head of the Beast, Yochanan sees one of the world powers that tried to annihilate Israel. Oddly enough, one dies and resurrects. Would this beast with the markings of every empire that persecuted his beloved country try to imitate Israel who also died and resurrected in the days of Jeremiah? Would Israel who recently died again resurrect? Will the empire that saw the death and resurrection of the Master, as well as conquered his country, also die and resurrect?

Yochanan watches with great dismay:

> They [the whole earth] worshipped the dragon, because he had given his authority to the beast; and they worshipped the beast, saying, "Who is like the beast? Who can fight against it?[144]

---

142. Rev 13:2
143. Rev 13:3
144. Rev 13:4

Yochanan is sickened at this praise to the Tanin, stolen from the liturgical psalm he uses in his daily prayers: "Who is like you, ADONAI, among the mighty? Who is like you, sublime in holiness, awesome in praises, working wonders?"[145]

> It was given a mouth speaking arrogant blasphemies; and it was given authority to act for forty-two months. So it opened its mouth in blasphemies against God to insult his name and his Sh'khinah, and those living in heaven.[146]

How the Roman Empire had already blasphemed! They burned the Temple on the Holy Mount to build instead a place of worship for the emperor. They killed the priests and persecuted those who did not yield to their ungodly demands.

> It was allowed to make war on God's holy people and to defeat them; and it was given authority over every tribe, people, language and nation.[147]

HaShem had given the authority to persecute his people. Yochanan remembers the Master's warning as he cried over Jerusalem:

> If you only knew today what is needed for shalom! But for now it is hidden from your sight. For the days are coming upon you when your enemies will set up a barricade around you, encircle you, hem you in on every side, and dash you to the ground, you and your children within your walls, leaving not one stone standing on another — and all because you did not recognize your opportunity when God offered it![148]

Yochanan remembered how each year, in the winter months, he and his friends celebrated the feast of Chanukah. They always remembered how Antiochus Epiphanes came out of the Grecian Empire and, "opened his mouth in blasphemies against God to insult his name and his Sh'khinah,

145. Exod 15:11
146. Rev 13:5–6
147. Rev 13:7
148. Lu 19:41–44

and those living in heaven; and how he was allowed to make war on God's holy people and to defeat them."[149] Yochanan saw a repeat through the Roman Empire, but wondered, "Could another leader come who could be even worse than those we have already seen?"

> Everyone living on earth will worship it except those whose names are written in the Book of Life belonging to the Lamb slaughtered before the world was founded. Those who have ears, let them hear! "If anyone is meant for captivity, into captivity he goes! If anyone is to be killed with the sword, with the sword he is to be killed!" This is when God's holy people must persevere and trust![150]

"Praise Yah!" Not all will fall. From the time when the lamb was slaughtered, even before the earth itself was created on the second day of creation, a faithful remnant is decreed to remain. A first fruit by which the whole "batch" is made holy!

> Then I saw another beast coming up out of the earth. It had two horns like those of a lamb, but it spoke like a dragon.[151]

This beast looks like a lamb, but it speaks the words of the Tanin. A dragon in sheep's clothing! Not only does it speak like the Tanin, but:

> It exercises all the authority of the first beast in its presence; and it makes the earth and its inhabitants worship the first beast, the one whose fatal wound had been healed. It performs great miracles, even causing fire to come down from heaven onto the earth as people watch. It deceives the people living on earth by the miracles it is allowed to perform in the presence of the beast.[152]

Yochanan remembers the words of the Master concerning HaSatan being a liar and a deceiver. Would it be surprising then for this human representative of the Tanin-inspired beastly government leader, the Anti-Messiah, to appear having two horns like a lamb so he could, as

149. Rev 13:5--7
150. Rev 13:8–10
151. Rev 13:11
152. Rev 13:12–14

Daniel saw, try to deceive the very elect? A lie is most toxic and lethal when it is closest to the truth. Yeshua knew about HaSatan. He said:

> When he tells a lie, he is speaking in character; because he is a liar — indeed, the inventor of the lie![153]

He comes on the world's scene as a wolf in sheep's clothing. He comes in hopes to deceive the weak, the simple, and those who have no depth, who only judge by outward appearance.

In his time, as shepherd of HaShem's flock, Yochanan has seen many false prophets. Their weapon is an outward show of piety and obedience. They speak the right words. They stand for the right things. They promote the right ideas. They portray themselves as liberators. They make promises of plenty and greatness in the name of right, but it is all pretenses in order to deceive those whose faith lacks depth and are easily deceived by rhetoric and outward appearances, who are easily fooled by the miracles of a preacher or politician.

Paul used to refer to these latter ones as some who "retain the outer form of religion but deny its power."[154] King David said of such people, "What he said sounded smoother than butter, but his heart was at war. His words seemed more soothing than oil, but in fact they were sharp swords."[155] The Master's words of warning come to him now:

> For there will appear false Messiahs and false prophets performing great miracles — amazing things! — so as to fool even the chosen, if possible.[156]

Yochanan is not surprised when he sees this impostor impersonate the true Messiah through miracles, many of them similar to those of the Master himself or that of the patriarchs and prophets of the Sacred Texts. What else could effectively deceive believers that their Messiah had returned? But Yeshua had warned them:

153. Jn 8:44
154. 2 Tim 3:5
155. Ps 55:21
156. Mt 24:24

> There! I have told you in advance! So if people say to you, "Listen! He's out in the desert!" Don't go; or, "Look! He's hidden away in a secret room!" Don't believe it. For when the Son of Man does come, it will be like lightning that flashes out of the east and fills the sky to the western horizon. (Mt 24:24–27)

To his great disappointment, Yochanan sees many who fall for the counterfeit. Just as those who receive Messiah receive the Father who gives him authority, he who receives who the Talmud calls, *Sheker-Mashiach* שקר משיח, the anti- or counterfeit Mashiach, receives the Dragon, HaSatan.

Is it possible that so many would be deceived? Yochanan thinks back at his own youth when, to him, it was so obvious that Yeshua was the promised Messiah of Israel. So many in his beloved Galilee believed and followed, but in Judea, it was another story. At that time, just like in the days of Jeremiah, the Temple authorities were more anxious to follow the words of their own false priestly prophets than those of the true Messiah. As the people, spurned by their leaders, shouted in favor of Barabbas, the vision shows Yochanan a future people shouting in favor of one who deceives them with false promises of grandeur. As the vision unfolds, Yochanan ponders on his Master's words:

> I have come in my Father's name, and you don't accept me; if someone else comes in his own name, him you will accept.[157]

A very familiar scene now unfolds in front of Yochanan. Once the Counterfeit Messiah has fooled everyone into thinking that he is some sort of messianic figure come to save them from their political, economic, as well as religious dissension, the imposter shows his true colors as he attempts to usurp HaShem's throne in the Temple and replace it with an image. It is Chanukah all over again, when Antiochus erected a statue of himself in the Temple.

Yochanan doesn't know if he should rejoice at the fact that the third Temple is indeed rebuilt or mourn that again it is defiled by an impious power.

157. Jn 5:43

> And it tells them to make an image honoring the beast that was struck by the sword but came alive again.[158]

The "Beast" has an image erected invoking its victory over death; an attempt at copying the sign of Yeshua's messiahship: the resurrection This will be a test for the disciples. They will have to be walking close to Yeshua to discern the difference. Those who walk afar off will be fooled by the "miracles," the lamb-like horns, and the words as smooth as butter. Only those who walk close to the Master will be able to discern the difference.

> It was allowed to put breath into the image of the beast, so that the image of the beast could even speak; and it was allowed to cause anyone who would not worship the image of the beast to be put to death.[159]

These words evoke in Yochanan the chilling memories of the days when, after the burning and destruction of the Jerusalem Temple, people were forced to worship Titus' image.

Yochanan remembers the chilling prophecies from the prophet Daniel who spoke of that terrible beast:

> Then I wanted to know what the fourth beast meant, the one that was different from all the others, so very terrifying, with iron teeth and bronze nails, which devoured, crushed and stamped its feet on what was left; … I watched, and that horn made war with the holy ones and was winning, … 'The fourth animal will be a fourth kingdom on earth. It will be different from the other kingdoms; it will devour the whole earth, trample it down and crush it. As for the ten horns, out of this kingdom ten kings will arise; and yet another will arise after them….He will speak words against the Most High and try to exhaust the holy ones of the Most High. He will attempt to alter the seasons and the law; and [the holy ones] will be handed over to him for a time, times and half a time.[160]

158. Rev 13:14
159. Rev 13:15
160. Dan 7:19–25

For three and half years, the brethren will have to suffer under the tyrant dictator who, like Antiochus Epiphanes and Titus, waged war against HaShem. Yochanan, who knew of the last jubilee set of years of man's rule on earth, also recalled Daniel's prophecy of a great, end-time evil ruler who somehow had the power to stop the daily sacrifice at the Jerusalem Temple. The Temple will surely be rebuilt, but would it be by a power that reserved itself some rights over it?

> He [*sheker-mashiach*] will make a strong covenant with leaders for one week [of years]. For half of the week he will put a stop to the sacrifice and the grain offering.[161]

The words of his friend Paul, who had been executed by Nero the current evil dictator, come to his mind:

> Don't let anyone deceive you in any way. For the Day will not come until after the Apostasy has come and the man who separates himself from Torah has been revealed, the one destined for doom. He will oppose himself to everything that people call a god or make an object of worship; he will put himself above them all, so that he will sit in the Temple of God and proclaim that he himself is God.[162]

As HaShem blew breath in the man he had created in his image to be his mouthpiece, the Tanin put words in the mouth of his image through his human government representative. The images of Rome's take-over of Jerusalem are still fresh in his mind and will help Yochanan understand what will happen again at the end of days. "Will there be a time again when a ruthless dictator will try to control the Temple worship and force our brothers and sisters to worship another deity?" he wonders.

> Also it forces everyone — great and small, rich and poor, free and slave — to receive a mark on his right hand or on his forehead preventing anyone from buying or selling unless he has the mark, that is, the name of the beast or the number of its name.[163]

161. Dan 9:27
162. 2 Thes 2:3–4
163. Rev 13:16–18

How many times will he resort to the same trick? An identity mark obtained by a profession of allegiance to the Roman government? Without this mark, one cannot be part of society. Yochanan had already seen how this affected the communities in the Diaspora. To invite someone to the fellowship of the believers was an invitation to social suicide. If they dedicated themselves to following and being disciples of Yeshua, they lost all social clout, economic edge, and even some of the necessities of life. True were the words of warning the apostle from Tarsus gave to his protégé Timothy: "All who want to live a godly life united with the Messiah Yeshua will be persecuted."[164]

Persecution was the way of life of the believers in those days. The disciples, the real ones who had profound love for Yeshua and whose faith was about establishing HaShem's Kingdom on earth through their lives, or deaths, were so strong. The world was not worthy of them!"[165]

Antiochus forbade the Jews to practice elements of Torah obedience, but this "Beast" pokes fun at *tefillin*, the leather boxes Jews set on their forehead and arms when they pray. Morning and evening, Yochanan dons his own tefillin. He uses small thin ones as the Master suggested, so not to make a show of religion.[166] With the head tefillin, he committed his will to HaShem. With the hand tefillin, he committed his actions to HaShem. Now this Tanin-inspired evil beast also wants his followers to commit their thoughts and actions to him under pain of death. "What a travesty!" Yochanan thinks in his own words.

> This is where wisdom is needed; those who understand should count the number of the beast, for it is the number of a person, and its number is 666.[167]

Yochanan was familiar with *Gematria*, or the system of counting the value of Hebrew words by adding the sum of their letters. He knew that Caesar Nero's Gematria equivalent was 666. How blessed

164. 2 Tim 3:12
165. Heb 11:35-38
166. Mt 23:5
167. Rev 13:17–18

will these people of the latter days be to be able to have this piece of information to identify this future tyrant!

The Lamb and the 144.000

Yochanan continues watching what unfolds before the great throne of the Almighty.

> Then I looked, and there was the Lamb standing on Mount Tziyon; and with him were 144,000 who had his name and his Father's name written on their foreheads.[168]

Yochanan sees the 12,000 from each of the tribes of Israel again.

> I heard a sound from heaven like the sound of rushing waters and like the sound of pealing thunder; the sound I heard was also like that of harpists playing on their harps.[169]

He hears, water, harps, and many other sounds.

> I heard the sound of their wings when they moved; it was like the sound of rushing water, like the voice of Shaddai, like the noise of a tumultuous crowd or army.[170]

> They were singing a new song before the throne and before the four living beings and the elders, and no one could learn the song except the 144,000 who have been ransomed from the world.[171]

David spoke of that new song: Sing a new song to ADONAI, because he has done wonders.[172] Yochanan sees these 144,000 faithful who have stayed close and did not compromise with the beast and its demands; those who follow closely wherever the Master goes.

> These are the ones who have not defiled themselves with women, for they are virgins; they follow the Lamb wherever he goes; they have

168. Rev 14:1
169. Rev 14:2
170. Ezek 1:24
171. Rev 14:3
172. Ps 98;1

> been ransomed from among humanity as first fruits for God and the Lamb; on their lips no lie was found — they are without defect.[173]

Messages of Good News

> Next I saw another angel flying in mid-heaven with everlasting Good News to proclaim to those living on the earth — to every nation, tribe, language and people.[174]
>
> Good news at last. The Kingdom must be at hand!
>
> In a loud voice he said, "Fear God, give him glory, for the hour has come when he will pass judgment! Worship the One who made heaven and earth, the sea and the springs of water!"[175]
>
> Finally! The moment all the prophets have foreseen and spoken about.
>
> Another angel, a second one, followed, saying, "She has fallen! She has fallen! Bavel the Great! She made all the nations drink the wine of God's fury caused by her whoring!"[176]

To avoid accusations of sedition, the disciples in the days of Yochanan referred to Rome as Bavel. Both Rome and Bavel were world powers who forced idolatry on the world; powers also that desecrated and destroyed the Jerusalem Holy Temple. Yochanan sees a latter-day Rome seeking control of the Temple to desecrate it; it already stopped the daily offerings. Yochanan remembers when Isaiah prophesied to the Children of Israel to leave Bavel before its destruction.

Another angel gives a final warning:

> Another angel, a third one, followed them and said in a loud voice, "If anyone worships the beast and its image and receives the mark on his forehead or on his hand, he will indeed drink the wine of

173. Rev 14:4–5
174. Rev 14:6
175. Rev 14:7
176. Rev 14:8

> God's fury poured undiluted into the cup of his rage. He will be tormented by fire and sulfur before the holy angels and before the Lamb, and the smoke from their tormenting goes up forever and ever. They have no rest, day or night, those who worship the beast and its image and those who receive the mark of its name." This is when perseverance is needed on the part of God's people, those who observe his commands and exercise Yeshua's faithfulness.[177]

This has been the goal of HaSatan from the very beginning: to steal the worship of mankind from HaShem and to bring humanity to that place of allegiance to him. Some partially succeeded, but all in the long-run, he always eventually failed. In this oracle, Yochanan hears the warning against those who fall in the trap of the deceiver. We are warned of the end of those who follow his deceptions.

The enemy of all righteousness comes to us lying and deceiving. From the very beginning, the instructions of the Torah have acted as a sort of litmus test against his deceptions. Yochanan remembers the beautiful words of King Solomon, "I found more bitter than death the woman who is a trap, whose heart is a snare and whose hands are like prison chains. The man who pleases God will escape from her, but the sinner will be caught by her."[178]

The Torah keeps us away from the snare of the fowler; the "evil woman," whose "house is the way to Sh'ol; ... down to the halls of death who lurks in the street corners to deceive us."

> Next I heard a voice from heaven saying, "Write: 'How blessed are the dead who die united with the Lord, from now on! Yes,' says the Spirit, 'now they may rest from their efforts, for the things they have accomplished follow along with them.'"[179]

Yochanan hears his Master's words

> How blessed are the poor in spirit! for the Kingdom of Heaven is theirs. How blessed are those who mourn! for they will be comforted.

177. Rev 14:8–12
178. Ecc 7:26
179. Rev 14:13

> How blessed are the meek! for they will inherit the Land! How blessed are those who hunger and thirst for righteousness! for they will be filled. How blessed are those who show mercy! for they will be shown mercy. How blessed are the pure in heart! for they will see God. How blessed are those who make peace! for they will be called sons of God. How blessed are those who are persecuted because they pursue righteousness! for the Kingdom of Heaven is theirs. How blessed you are when people insult you and persecute you and tell all kinds of vicious lies about you because you follow me! Rejoice, be glad, because your reward in heaven is great — they persecuted the prophets before you in the same way.[180]

Yochanan now rejoices. It has not been all in vain. Deliverance does come. The promises are fulfilled! He sees his Master on a white cloud, sickle in hand:

> The Harvest
>
> Then I looked, and there before me was a white cloud. Sitting on the cloud was someone like a Son of Man with a gold crown on his head and a sharp sickle in his hand. Another angel came out of the Temple and shouted to the one sitting on the cloud, "Start using your sickle to reap, because the time to reap has come — the earth's harvest is ripe!" The one sitting on the cloud swung his sickle over the earth, and the earth was harvested.[181]

It is Sukkot, five days after Yom Kippur. As the time of the last harvests of the year come, Yochanan sees the final great harvest of humanity. As the fruit of the season is gathered into barns, the faithful are gathered unto Messiah. Yochanan remembers the words of the Master concerning the last harvest, as well as those of his dear colleague Paul, now passed on: "For the Lord himself will come down from heaven with a rousing cry, with a call from one of the ruling angels, and with God's shofar; those who died united with the Messiah will be the first to rise; then we who are left still alive will be caught up with them in

180. Mat 5:3–12

181. Rev 14:14–15

the clouds to meet the Lord in the air; and thus we will always be with the Lord. So encourage each other with these words."[182]

Yochanan sees another harvester

> Another angel came out of the Temple in heaven, and he too had a sharp sickle. Then out from the altar went yet another angel, who was in charge of the fire; and he called in a loud voice to the one with the sharp sickle, "Use your sharp sickle, and gather the clusters of grapes from the earth's vine, because they are ripe!" The angel swung his sickle down onto the earth, gathered the earth's grapes and threw them into the great winepress of God's fury. The winepress was trodden outside the city, and blood flowed from the winepress as high as the horses' bridles for two hundred miles![183]

Judgment had surely started with the House of HaShem. His children safely rescued, now the time has come for the great judgment: the tribulation of those who persecuted HaShem's children. In awe and great expectancy, Yochanan watches as the vision continues to unfold.

182. 1 Thes 4:16–18
183. Rev 14:18–20

Chapter 5
Seven Bowls Of Wrath

- God's Fury Unleashed
- A Look behind the Scene
- The Judgment of the Great Whore

God's Fury Unleashed

> Then I saw another sign in heaven, a great and wonderful one — seven angels with the seven plagues that are the final ones; because with them, God's fury is finished.[1]

The six random shofars foretold of the tribulation that is coming to the believers; "to those who obey God's commands and bear witness to Yeshua."[2] Yochanan is familiar with Jacob's trouble before the great deliverance.[3] He also remembers that HaShem called his people out before he was ready to pour his judgments upon Bavel.[4]

The futuristic vision continues to reveal HaShem's great plan. Not only will his children, exiled because of their sins, experience a deliverance that will pale with that of the Exodus from Egypt.[5] As happened with all the great nations of the past which persecuted them, they will see the judgement of their redeemer upon their persecutors. Yochanan remembers the praises of the song of Moshe and Miriam's dance with the women:[6]

1. Rev 15:1
2. Rev 12:17
3. Jer 30:3-7
4. Isa 48:12–20; Rev 14:6-16
5. Jer 23:7–8
6. Exod 15:1-21

> I saw what looked like a sea of glass mixed with fire.[7]

Was this the sea of glass that Moshe, Aaron and his children, as well as the 70 elders saw as they ate with HaShem?[8] Yochanan feels honored to also partake with all that these great saints of Jewish history have witnessed.

> Those defeating the beast, its image and the number of its name were standing by the sea of glass, holding harps which God had given them.[9]

Yochanan cannot help but think of the great warrior, King David, who sang of HaShem's victorious acts accompanying his praises with his harp.

> They were singing the song of Moshe, the servant of God, and the song of the Lamb: "Great and wonderful are the things you have done, ADONAI, God of heaven's armies! Just and true are your ways, king of the nations! ADONAI, who will not fear and glorify your name? because you alone are holy. All nations will come and worship before you, for your righteous deeds have been revealed."[10]

Standing and taking part in this great heavenly service that he entered at the beginning of the vision, Yochanan hears the words of the song Moshe. These same words are usually repeated during the synagogue and Temple services. Yochanan hears those who came out of the last exile, the Roman exile, sing the same song that Moshe and the children of Israel sang when they came out of the Egyptian exile. He hears them also as they learn and sing the song of the Lamb.

> After this I looked, and the sanctuary (that is, the Tent of Witness in heaven) was opened, and out of the sanctuary came the seven angels with the seven plagues. They were dressed in clean bright linen and had gold belts around their chests. One of the four living beings gave to the seven angels seven gold bowls filled with the fury of God, who lives forever and ever.[11]

7. Rev 15:2
8. Exod 24:9–11
9. Rev 15:2
10. Rev 15:3–4
11. Rev 15:5–7

Every Yom Kippur, Yochanan imagined what it would be like to actually see heaven open, the heavenly sanctuary, and the Ark of God. Now he sees what the yearly rehearsals of the fall feasts were all about: the final judgment. After great trials and tribulations, the believers are finally rescued and comforted in the company of their redeemer. Now, as he took personal responsibility to execute judgement upon the Egyptians,[12] angels come out from his throne carrying bowls of plagues against those who troubled his children.

> Then the sanctuary was filled with smoke from God's Sh'khinah, that is, from his power; and no one could enter the sanctuary until the seven plagues of the seven angels had accomplished their purpose.[13]

Something else has to happen before the restoration of all things.

> I heard a loud voice from the sanctuary say to the seven angels, "Go, and pour out on the earth the seven bowls of God's fury!" (Rev 16:1)

The beast and its minions had been allowed to open their mouths "in blasphemies against God, to insult his name and his Sh'khinah, and those living in heaven. They were allowed to make war on God's holy people and to defeat them; given authority over every tribe, people, language and nation."[14] Now he responds to these souls under the altar crying, "Sovereign Ruler, *HaKadosh*, the True One, how long will it be before you judge the people living on earth and avenge our blood?"[15]

In response to all the martyrs that have been, are, and will be, HaShem, the great vindicator of his people, the rewarder of every innocent victim of the injustice and cruelty of man against man, comes out in fury, great vengeance, and deliverance.

Yochanan remembers the words of the Master when he compared those days to the days of Noah. Noah's family was rescued, being taken up by the waters of the flood while HaShem's judgments poured out onto the earth, only to return after the water receded. As such, it

12. Exod 12:13
13. Rev 15:8
14. Rev 13:6-7
15. Rev 6:10

is a great comfort to Yochanan to have seen the family of believers, those who have suffered so much for the Name of the Master, also taken up[16] to safety and security before judgment starts falling on those who persecuted them.

> So the first one went and poured his bowl onto the earth, and disgusting and painful sores appeared on all the people who had the mark of the beast and worshipped its image. The second one poured out his bowl into the sea, and it became like the blood of a dead person, and every living thing in the sea died. The third one poured out his bowl into the rivers and springs of water, and they turned to blood. (Rev 16:2–4)

Sores and waters turned to blood; the plagues of Egypt all over again. The first and the second redemptive act: the first as a blueprint for the second. As in the days of the last plague of Egypt, when HaShem's judgments spared the houses of those who had the "mark of the lamb" on the doorposts of their houses, so this time, the plagues affect only those who had received the mark of the beast.

> Then I heard the angel of the waters say... (Rev 16:5)

Yochanan had been introduced to the angel of the Abyss,[17] as well as the angel in charge of the fire.[18] Now he hears the angel who, he was told, rebelled: the angel of the waters,[19] who accepts his bloody judgment and, in all humility, proclaims:

> O HaKadosh[20], the One who is and was, you are just in these judgments of yours. They poured out the blood of your people and your prophets, so you have made them drink blood. They deserve it! (Rev 16:5–6)

16. Rev 14:14–16

17. Rev 9:11

18. Rev 14:18

19. Jewish teachings say that God employed the angel of the sea to swallow up the waters at the creation; that the dry land might appear. He disobeyed, and God slew him; the name of the angel of the sea is Rahab. See Baba bathra, fol. 74, 2.

20. In Hebrew, HaKadosh, short for *HaKadosh Baruch Huh* הקדוש ברוך הוא, used interchangeably for Hashem and for Messiah.

In awe and wonder, Yochanan remembers Isaiah's prophecy about those who fight against HaShem's children being made to drink their own blood.[21] The angel in charge of fire in the altar of the Temple concurs.[22]

> Then I heard the altar say, "Yes, ADONAI, God of heaven's armies, your judgments are true and just!" (Rev 16:7)

> The fourth one poured out his bowl on the sun, and it was permitted to burn people with fire. People were burned by the intense heat; yet they cursed the name of God, who had the authority over these plagues, instead of turning from their sins to give him glory. (Rev 16:8–9)

Just as in the days of Egypt, the hearts of the people become hard. "How is it," Yochanan thinks, "that man can go through plagues, natural or man-made disasters, wars, troubles of all sorts, and be able to rationalize it so as to never come to the realization that they are fighting against the God of the universe, against whom they cannot win? Is arrogance so delusional?" He remembers how, until the end, the Egyptian Pharaoh continued his relentless fight against the God of Israel.

> The fifth one poured out his bowl on the throne of the beast, and its kingdom grew dark. People gnawed on their tongues from the pain, yet they cursed the God of heaven because of their pains and sores, and did not turn from their sinful deeds. (Rev 16:10–11)

HaSatan himself reminded Yeshua that the kingdoms of the world had been handed to him, and that consequently, he could give them to whomsoever he wanted.[23] From the Pharaohs of Egypt to the Caesars of Rome, the demonic leaders of all the dominating powers of the earth have had their centers, their palaces where they sat on their thrones as the gods of the earth, sometimes even presiding over a pantheon of gods. Yochanan now sees pain caused by sores; a plagues not seen since the days of Egypt affecting what will be the throne of the beast, the ruling center of Daniel's resurrected fourth kingdom..

21. Isa 49:25–26
22. Rev 14:18
23. Lu 4:6

He remembers Egypt when, even though the last plague personally affected Pharaoh through the loss of his own first-born, he who was meant to be "god-on-earth" in his stead, Pharaoh continued in his rebellious attitude and hardening of his heart. In the same manner, the kingdom of the demonic beast sees disaster after disaster at the hand of the Almighty God of Israel, and yet does not submit. This is the difference between the righteous and the rebels. While suffering brings the righteous to repentance, it fosters more rebellion in him who is predisposed to insubordination.[24]

> The sixth one poured out his bowl on the great river Euphrates, and its water dried up, in order to prepare the way for the kings from the east. (Rev 16:12)

Like the prophets of the Babylonian exile, Yochanan understands his vision in relation to the fate of Israel and of Jerusalem. In their days, Daniel sought to know the numbers of years of the exile; Ezekiel sought to understand what brought on the exile, and Jeremiah exposed the spiritual and historical events that provoked it. Now, Yochanan plays the role of them all. He witnesses the subjugation of Israel, the destruction of Jerusalem and of its great Temple. He sees the last great exile of his people and he asks questions. "Why, how long, who, what, where, and when?"

As in the days of Antiochus Epiphanes of the eastern Grecian Empire of Syria, those who came to stop the daily sacrifice[25] assemble for war. As in the time of the Seleucid kings' struggle for dominance, Israel is bracing to become the battle field of a cosmic battle.[26] Empire after empire has tried to dominate Israel, but history testifies that Israel is HaShem's firstborn son and none but HaShem can rule over him.

A Look Behind the Scene

As the vision unfolds, Yochanan is given intelligence as to the origin of these empirical powers. He discovers the spiritual source behind this great assembly of armies coming against the Land.

24. 2 Cor 7:10
25. Dan 9:27
26. Dan 11

> And I saw three unclean spirits that looked like frogs; they came from the mouth of the dragon, from the mouth of the beast and from the mouth of the false prophet. They are miracle-working demonic spirits which go out to the kings of the whole inhabited world to assemble them for the War of the Great Day of ADONAI-Tzva'ot. (Rev 16:13–14)

The dragon, the beast, and the false prophet have one mind and speak as one. In typical Semitic imagery, HaShem shows Yochanan unclean spirits coming out of their mouths. Their voices are raw and croaky. Their words come from the bottom of the slimiest pond. Their rhetoric is born of puffed up pride with just the pretense of substance. The three have the same goals: the possession of both HaShem's assembly and of the Land he calls his own. Like Antiochus IV, they come to fight against HaShem.

Intelligence keeps flowing into Yochanan, who listens and watches attentively.

> Look! I am coming like a thief! How blessed are those who stay alert and keep their clothes clean, so that they won't be walking naked and be publicly put to shame! (Rev 16:15)

Using the familiar language of the Oral Torah, the Talmudic traditions, the oracle identifies the season of these events. Due to its arrival on the first of Tishri, Yom Teruah[27] has always been the day that comes like a thief. Paul, the emissary, taught the disciples in Thessalonica about events concerning the latter-days, using the same language.[28]

Because of the uncertain day of its arrival, people in Israel had to be ready for the festivals of the disappearing moon of Elul. Those who were diligent had their white garment ready, as well as their food for the festivals. Those who did not were caught unaware as the new moon of Tishri appeared.

Now, Yochanan knows who, when, why, how long, and how. He just needs to know where:

27. Rosh Hashanah
28. 1Thes 5

> And they gathered the kings to the place which in Hebrew is called Har Megiddo. (Rev 16:16)

"Of course!" Yochanan thinks. He remembers learning about all the famous historical battles in this valley, called by some, Armageddon, known as "the ideal battleground." He remembers as a child watching the Jezreel Valley from the hills of his beloved Galilee, dreaming about his favorite heroes. He could think of Deborah and Barak against Sisera with the stars fighting on their behalf,[29] of Saul against the Philistines,[30] of Solomon against Pharaoh Shishak[31] and of King Josiah against Pharaoh Necho.[32] He couldn't imagine all of the wars that would eventually be fought in that valley, including those leading to the latter-days when General George Allenby fought against the Ottoman Turks in 1918, and when Kibbutz Mishmar Ha'emek fought the Arab Liberation Army in 1948. Of course, this is where the last battle against Israel will take place. Every year, at the time of Sukkot he had read about the great battle in the scroll of Ezekiel[33]. Now he is seeing it with his own eyes!

The Judgment of the Great Whore

> The seventh one poured out his bowl on the air, and a loud voice came out of the Temple from the throne, saying, "It is done!" There were flashes of lightning, voices and peals of thunder; and there was a massive earthquake, such as has never occurred since mankind has been on earth, so violent was the earthquake. (Rev 16:17–18)

The drama in the vision keeps unfolding, culminating in a great and awesome event. Lightning, thunder, and earthquakes all remind Yochanan of the events at mount Horeb, as well the time of the crucifixion of the Master. What is to happen this time?

---

29. Judg 5
30. 1 Sam 31
31. 2 Chron 12:3–4
32. 2 Kings 23:29
33. Ezek 38–39

> The great city was split into three parts, the cities of the nations fell, and God remembered Bavel the Great and made her drink the wine from the cup of his raging fury. (Rev 16:19)

The day of reckoning has come for that great city that persecuted the seed of the woman, the believers. As she had treated them, so she was treated. The violence she has poured on others is now poured upon her.

> Every island fled, and no mountains were to be found. And huge seventy-pound hailstones fell on people from the sky. But the people cursed God for the plague of hail, that it was such a terrible plague. (Rev 16:20–21)

Yochanan remembers the words of the dear prophets who, unknown to them, spoke about this day.[34] An angel addresses Yochanan:

> Then came one of the angels with the seven bowls; and he said to me, "Come, I will show you the judgment of the great whore who is sitting by many waters. (Rev 17:1)

The "Great Whore." Many cities, mostly commercial centers of the ancient world, are given that appellation in the Tanakh: Nineveh, Tyre, Babylon, and even Jerusalem in her idolatrous days.[35] Yeshua warned the disciples about the potential incompatibilities between service to HaShem and dedication to commercial ventures.[36]

> The kings of the earth went whoring with her, and the people living on earth have become drunk from the wine of her whoring. (Rev 17:2)

Yochanan is familiar with these centers of idolatry that make up the Greco-Roman world. Entire nations become dependent on their trade, but in that world, even commercial ventures are religious and there is no trade without blessing the gods of the city. Man was created to seek protection and sufficiency from the God that made him, but these cities of trade presented their wares under the banner of the gods of

34. Hag 2:6-7; (Isa 24:19–21
35. Nah 3:4; Isa 23:17; Isa 1:21; Ezek 16;
36. Mt 6:24

Greece and Rome. Bala'am of old provoked only Israel to idolatry,[37] but these cities provoked entire nations to idolatry, inciting them to do commerce with her. For fine fabric, exotic spices, and sweet wine, they sold their souls.

> He carried me off in the Spirit to a desert, and I saw a woman sitting on a scarlet beast filled with blasphemous names and having seven heads and ten horns. (Rev 17:3)

Yochanan, again, is invited to see events which transcend time and space. Like Daniel, he sees them without the veil that would hide their spiritual nature to the naked eye. He sees the dragon. He sees the empires the dragon rules over. He sees the beast of the latter-days, and he sees the city of the beast, the place where his throne resides. She is called Egypt, Tyre, Nineveh, Babylon, Athens, and Rome. "Is there another one?" he wonders. "Is there another harlot who like the strange woman[38]will use her charms and cunning wiles to lead the sons of man away from the true God? Is there another one who will commit this ultimate blasphemy?"

> The woman was dressed in purple and scarlet and glittered with gold, precious stones and pearls. In her hand was a gold cup filled with the obscene and filthy things produced by her whoring. On her forehead was written a name with a hidden meaning, Bavel the Great Mother of Whores and of the Earth's obscenities. (Rev 17:4–5)

As the beast that rose out of the sea[39] is the antithesis of the Kingdom of God on earth; as the other beast coming up out of the earth who had two horns like a lamb but spoke as a dragon is the antithesis of Messiah; this mother of whores and of the earth's obscenities is the antithesis of the ultimate pure and holy bride Jerusalem, the city of the great King. She is the loose woman, the adulteress, glancing out through the lattice, bent on deceiving the simple who do not read through her evil charms. Many are those she has struck down dead, numerous those she has killed. In their simple-mindedness, they did

37. Jude 1:11
38. Prov 7:5–27
39. Rev 13:1

not perceive that her house is the way to Sh'ol; that it leads down to the halls of death.[40]

> I saw the woman drunk from the blood of God's people, that is, from the blood of the people who testify about Yeshua. (Rev 17:6)

Those who do commerce with her do so at the cost of their souls. Many succumb to her charms and find themselves trapped. Those whom she cannot control and bow to her gods, she kills. She is drunk; yes, she is drunk from the blood of the martyrs of all generations; from all the innocent blood that has ever been shed on earth, from the blood of innocent Hevel to the blood of Z'kharyah Ben-Berekhyah, whom you murdered between the Temple and the altar.[41] She is drunk also from the blood of his dear friends and colleagues; the blood of all the followers of the Master all throughout the Roman empire; yes, even with the blood of those that Yochanan sees in his vision of the altar,[42] and even those who she will kill up to the blessed day of the returning of the Master.

In her, Yochanan sees Cain who killed his righteous brother out of jealousy; Pharaoh and his evil decree;[43] Saul bent on killing David.[44] He sees every empire who pushed their idolatrous religious system onto Israel to make them sin before their God, from the days of the creation of the earth till the end of times.

> On seeing her, I was altogether astounded. Then the angel said to me, "Why are you astounded? I will tell you the hidden meaning of the woman and of the beast with seven heads and ten horns that was carrying her.[45]

Yochanan is astounded. The angel, that seems to be his guide, explains to him.

---

40. Prov 7:5–27
41. Mt 23:25
42. Rev 6:9–11
43. Exod 1:22
44. 1 Sam 18
45. Rev 17:6–7

> The beast you saw once was, now is not, and will come up from the Abyss; but it is on its way to destruction.[46]

Yochanan receives a quick summary of immediate upcoming history. He learns that the beast, that fourth kingdom in Daniel's prophecy[47]that represents the Roman Empire, will eventually disappear from the scene of world dominations, to once again rise from the abyss of the masses. Yochanan is amazed as he ponders HaShem's sense of historical order. He thinks of his Master appearing on the world scene, disappearing, only to reappear in the latter-days. Such will seem to be the fate of his own country, Israel, who appeared, then disappeared under Rome, only to reappear in the latter-days This happens alongside a new reappearing "Rome," the kingdom of the beast who tries to annihilate her but who this time is on the way to destruction while conquered and outlived by Israel and her Messiah.[48]

> The people living on earth whose names have not been written in the Book of Life since the founding of the world will be astounded to see the beast that once was, now is not, but is to appear.[49]

What blasphemy is in the mouth of those who are astounded at the beast, and what ultimate low trickery to try to deceive humanity by identifying with the Holy One whom Yochanan prays to as, "He Who Was, Is, and is to Come," *hu hayah v'hu hoveh v'hu yihyeh* הוא היה והוא אווה והוא יהיה.

The disciples, those who have the seal of HaShem and of the Lamb on their forehead have been taken away[50] to rest from the intense tribulation they received at the hand of the beast and those who bear his mark[51]. There are many other people, whole nations left on earth and who live under the tyrannical rule of this cosmic devilish power. These people marvel at its ability to appear on the world scene, disappear, and then reappear.

46. Rev 17:8
47. Dan 7: 7-8; 19–28
48. Dan 2:44–45
49. Rev 17:8
50. Rev 14;14–16
51. Rev 6:9–11

Yochanan continues listening to the oracle.

> This calls for a mind with wisdom: the seven heads are seven hills on which the woman is sitting; also they are seven kings—five have fallen, one is living now and the other is yet to come; and when he does come, he must remain only a little while.[52]

Yochanan's mind races back to the prophecies of the Daniel. Seven empires embodied by seven major world leaders were the instruments of persecution of Israel: Egypt, Assyria, Babylon, Persia, Greece, and now Rome. Five have come and gone, but Rome, the sixth one, continues even in the days of Yochanan. To his horror, Yochanan sees another persecution in the far away future of Israel. So many persecutions! So many die for the Name of HaShem! "After all this with the Romans, will there be another holocaust?" he wonders. "Is this our destiny as the chosen people?" Is this what it means to be the "first fruit of humanity?"[53] Are we believers that first fruit that is to be offered on the altar to represent the whole harvest? Are we the first fruit representative of humanity?[54] Will there be a first fruit representative of each generation until the return of our dear Master? Please come soon, even in our days!" Yochanan prays. "It is hardly bearable to conceive!"

> The beast which once was and now is not is an eighth king; it comes from the seven and is on its way to destruction.[55]

"Seven was not enough? Now an eighth one, coming from the seventh? When will it end, Lord?" Yochanan prays as he continues watching, expecting answers concerning the description of the beast.

> The ten horns you saw are ten kings who have not yet begun to rule, but they receive power as kings for one hour, along with the beast. They have one mind, and they hand over their power and authority to the beast.[56]

52. Rev 17:9–10
53. Rev 14:14
54. Rom 11:16
55. Rev 17:11
56. Rev 17:12

Yochanan learns that the number ten represents a complete congregation, body, or kingdom, whether good or evil.[57] "The beast gives power and authority to the kings of the world for a little time. The beast, who already stopped the daily sacrifice[58], wants to take HaShem's place in the Temple. Will the Temple be destroyed again? Is that why they all come to make war on Israel at the Valley of Har-Megiddo? No, it cannot be!"

57.

- There are Ten Commandments;
- Ten Plagues
- Abraham endured 10 trials.
- For the sake of 10 righteous people, YHWH would have spared Sodom. (Gen. 18)
- Abraham's servant brought 10 camels as gifts to Rebecca. He knew she was the one because she watered them. (Gen, 24) Her brother (Laban) and her mother wanted her tarry with them for ten days. Could these represent the 10 Words and what helps us (the bride) to endure the wilderness until we meet our Groom?
- Laban changed Jacob's wages ten times. (Gen. 31:7)
- Ten of Joseph's brothers had to go down to Egypt to buy grain because of famine. (Gen. 42:3) Joseph sent them back with ten donkeys loaded with goods and ten female donkeys loaded with grain. (Gen, 45:23)
- Israel rebelled 10 times in the wilderness. (Num. 14:22)
- Israelites gathered at least 10 homers of quail in the wilderness. Those that ate it died with the meat between their teeth. (Num. 11:32)
- There were 10 of 12 spies that gave a bad report to Israel, costing them forty more years (4 x 10) in the wilderness.
- Foundation of Tabernacle was made from 10 x 10 silver sockets.
- Fire came down from heaven 10 times (6 were in judgment).
- Boaz sat before ten men (elders/rulers) at the city gate to redeem the field of Naomi (Elimelech) and to also take Ruth as his wife to carry on the name of his deceased relative (Levirate marriage), Mahlon. (Ruth 4)
- Ten Virgins (5 wise, 5 foolish).
- Ten lost tribes of Israel.
- Wicked Haman had ten sons. (Est 9:12)
- Tenth generation represented whole. (Deut. 23:3)
- Ten generations from Adam to Noah.
- Minyan is made complete with 10 men.
- Ten Days of Awe between Rosh Hashanah and Yom Kippur.
- Day of Atonement falls on 10th day of Tishrei.
- In the Parable of the Lost Coin (Lu 15:8–10), the woman has a total of ten silver coins. (Silver is the metal/color of redemption.) When she loses one, she lights a lamp and sweeps the HOUSE, until she finds the lost coin. Then, she and the entire community rejoices with her.
- The beast that the harlot rides in Revelation has 7 heads and ten horns as does the fourth beast in Daniel's night visions (Dan.7). The horns represent wicked kings or rulers.
- Using the number 10, HaShem show Zechariah the prophet that there will come a time when all Gentile nations will grab onto the tzitzit of the Jewish Messiah in order to obtain his covering: ADONAI-Tzva'ot says, "When that time comes, ten men will take hold — speaking all the languages of the nations — will grab hold of the cloak of a Jew and say, 'We want to go with you, because we have heard that God is with you'." (Zech 8:23)

58. Dan 9:27

> They will go to war against the Lamb.[59]

The beast engages the nations of the world to fight against the Lamb:

> But the Lamb will defeat them, because he is Lord of lords and King of kings, and those who are called, chosen and faithful will overcome along with him.[60]

"Halleluyah!" Exclaims Yochanan. The angel/guide provides more information on the judgment of the "whore."

> Then he said to me, "The waters that you saw, where the whore is sitting, are peoples, crowds, nations and languages. As for the ten horns that you saw and the beast, they will hate the whore, bring her to ruin, leave her naked, eat her flesh and consume her with fire."[61]

Like one who rejects a prostitute after he has made use of her to satisfy his own urges, the world turns against that great city. The nations destroy her who sat upon the beast.

> For God put it in their hearts to do what will fulfill his purpose, that is, to be of one mind and give their kingdom to the beast until God's words have accomplished their intent. And the woman you saw is the great city that rules over the kings of the earth.[62]

The world destroys the city that was drunk from the blood of HaShem's saints. Unknown to them, HaShem always leads the nations to do his bidding. He used Babylon to judge Jerusalem and used Persia to judge Babylon.

A bright, shiny angel arrives on the scene to make an announcement:

> After these things, I saw another angel coming down from heaven. He had great authority, the earth was lit up by his splendor. He cried out in a strong voice, "She has fallen! She has fallen! Bavel the Great! She has become a home for demons, a prison for every unclean spirit, a prison for every unclean, hated bird. For all

59. Rev 17:14
60. Rev 17:14
61. Rev 17:15–16
62. Rev 17:17–18

> the nations have drunk of the wine of God's fury caused by her whoring — yes, the kings of the earth went whoring with her, and from her unrestrained love of luxury the world's businessmen have grown rich."[63]

Babylon. Babylon who persecuted the disciples; Babylon who lived in opulence while disregarding the poor of the earth; Babylon who lured the nations of the earth to commit lewd lasciviousness has now been judged. She has been punished for her mammon worship through her greed and selfishness.[64] The black horse ran unrestrained through her land, causing the world to suffer in poverty.[65] Yochanan thinks of the warning against the wealthy city of Tyre,[66] whom he understands as a surrogate for the realm of HaSatan.

> Then I heard another voice out of heaven say: "My people, come out of her! so that you will not share in her sins, so that you will not be infected by her plagues, for her sins are a sticky mass piled up to heaven, and God has remembered her crimes.[67]

Yochanan remembers Lot and his family whom angels begged to leave the city before the judgment came down on Sodom and Gomorrah. He remembers how by the mouth of his faithful prophets, HaShem begged the children of Israel to leave the city of Babylon before the judgments fell.[68] The words of the Master, when he gave the disciples a sign to leave Jerusalem before its imminent destruction, are still fresh.[69] Again, HaShem calls his people out before judgments fall. Will they obey, or like Lot's sons-in-law, remain in the city? Will they leave in haste or turn back like Lot's wife?

> Render to her as she rendered to others! Pay her back double for what she has done! Use the cup in which she has brewed to brew her

63. Rev 18:1–3
64. 1 Tim 6:9–10
65. Rev 6:5–6
66. Ezek 28:11–19
67. Rev 18:4–5
68. Isa: 48:20; Jer: 1:8; Jer: 51:6, Jer: 51:45.
69. Lu 21:20–24

> a double-sized drink! Give her as much torment and sorrow as the glory and luxury she gave herself![70]

Yochanan thinks of *midah k'neged midah* מידה כנגד מידה or, "measure for measure," the main standard of judgment and retribution in the Torah. This principle teaches that at the end of days, we are treated the same way we have treated others and are judged using the same unit of measure we have used to judge others. His beloved Master and Rabbi, Yeshua, extensively taught about that. He said, "Don't judge, so that you won't be judged. For the way you judge others is how you will be judged — the measure with which you measure out will be used to measure to you"[71]. Yochanan also thinks of the parable of Lazarus, who was despised by the rich neighbor during his lifetime.[72] The oppressors of the earth will one day pay for their selfishness, pride, and indifference. They will themselves receive retribution by him who redeems the slave, the prisoner, and the oppressed in the day of the great jubilee to come.

> For in her heart she says, "I sit a queen — I am not a widow, I will never see sorrow."[73]

Filled with pride and arrogance, Babylon measures herself against Jerusalem who, in the days of Yochanan, had already become a widow, abused by every neighbor.[74]

> Therefore, her plagues will come in a single day - death, sorrow and famine; and she will be burned with fire, because ADONAI, God, her Judge, is mighty.[75]

Like Sodom and Gomorrah, her judgment comes suddenly. As a result, the merchants of the earth mourn; the rich and wealthy weep; the strong and mighty lament as their world is brought down.

70. Rev 18:6–7
71. Mt 7:1-2
72. Lu 16:19–31
73. Rev 18:7
74. Lam 1:1
75. Rev 18:8

> The kings of the earth who went whoring with her and shared her luxury will sob and wail over her when they see the smoke as she burns. Standing at a distance, for fear of her torment, they will say, "Oh no! The great city! Bavel, the mighty city! In a single hour your judgment has come!"[76]

Those who committed adultery by trading their merchandise with her are left alone with their riches and no-one to buy their wares.

> The world's businessmen weep and mourn over her, because no one is buying their merchandise any more—stocks of gold and silver, gems and pearls, fine linen and purple, silk and scarlet, all rare woods, all ivory goods, all kinds of things made of scented wood, brass, iron and marble; cinnamon, cardamom, incense, myrrh, frankincense, wine, oil, flour, grain, cattle, sheep, horses, chariots - and bodies - and people's souls.[77]

Where is their world now? Yeshua taught his disciples to not put their trust in uncertain riches and not work for the food which passes away.[78] The heavenly lament on Babylon reminds Yochanan of the message he received for the congregation in Laodicea, "For you keep saying, 'I am rich, I have gotten rich, I don't need a thing!' You don't know that you are the one who is wretched, pitiable, poor, blind and naked!" [79]

> The fruits you lusted for with all your heart have gone! All the luxury and flashiness have been destroyed, never to return! The sellers of these things, who got rich from her, will stand at a distance, for fear of her torment, weeping and mourning, and saying, "Oh no! The great city used to wear fine linen, purple and scarlet! She glittered with gold, precious stones and pearls! Such great wealth - in a single hour, ruined!"[80]

Those who cry for her, do they really cry for her, or do they cry for themselves?

---

76. Rev 18:9–10
77. Rev 18:11–13
78. Jn 6:27
79. Rev 3:17
80. Rev 18:14–17

> All the ship masters, passengers, sailors and everyone making his living from the sea stood at a distance and cried out when they saw the smoke as she burned, "What city was like the great city?" And they threw dust on their heads as they wept and mourned, saying, "Oh no! The great city! The abundance of her wealth made all the ship owners rich! In a single hour she is ruined!"[81]

Blinded by her luxury, deceived by her lies, and goaded by her mockery of all that is good and godly, those who entered business with her, who enjoyed the pleasure of sin for a season in her luxurious abodes were all in denial of the Faustian deal they were entering. They had forgotten the warning of the king of old, "For many are those she has struck down dead, numerous those she has killed. Her house is the way to Sh'ol; it leads down to the halls of death."[82]

But the lovers of the true Jerusalem who own the true riches which do not perish go on rejoicing, for their day has come. The life they hid underground in Messiah[83] will soon flourish above ground. From their place of rest,[84] those she has killed behold the judgment of the great whore. Like Lazarus,[85] they can only stand and watch the sorrow of those who, deceived,[86] put their trust in her perishing wealth.

> Rejoice over her, heaven! Rejoice, people of God, emissaries and prophets! For in judging her, God has vindicated you.[87]

Yochanan praises HaShem as the prayers of the martyrs of all ages are finally heard. This is the greatest fall festival of all, the jubilee of all jubilees, The Yom Teruah of Yom Teruahs, the Yom Kippur of Yom Kippurs. Judgment, vengeance, and vindication have finally come.

81. Rev 18:17–19
82. Prov 7:26–27
83. Col 3:3
84. Rev 6:9–11
85. Lu 16
86. 1 John 2:16
87. Rev 18:20

> Then a mighty angel picked up a boulder the size of a great millstone, and hurled it into the sea, saying, "With violence like this will the great city Bavel be hurled down, never to be found again!"[88]

"What a sight! Blessed be our mighty God who hears the prayers of his saints!" screams Yochanan. HaShem punished Sodom and Gomorrah in one hour; he can certainly punish Babylon in one hour.

> The sound of harpists and musicians, flute-players and trumpeters will never again be heard in you. No worker of any trade will ever again be found in you, the sound of a mill will never again be heard in you, the light of a lamp will never again shine in you, the voice of bridegroom and bride will never again be heard in you.[89]

The heavenly lament over Babylon seems to echo that of Jerusalem when it was widowed. She who boasted against Jerusalem saying, I am no widow, now reaps the harvest of her own iniquitous indulgence and pride. The laments he hears concerning Babylon remind Yochanan of Isaiah and Jeremiah, the prophets of the God who prophesied concerning Jerusalem.[90] She who boasted against Jerusalem is receiving herself the fruit of her own boasting.

> For your businessmen were the most powerful on earth, all the nations were deceived by your magic spell. "In her was found the blood of prophets and of God's people, indeed, of all who have ever been slaughtered on earth![91]

"What a warning for the congregation of Messiah that will live in those days," Yochanan ponders. He contemplates those days with the same apprehension that he presently feels over the family of believers in his own days. Many are deceived by the beast and the whore. Many do not follow the admonitions of the Master and of his emissaries to not be tempted by the oldest of all temptations.[92] They do not even follow those he himself gave saying, "Do not love the world or the

88. Rev 18:21
89. Rev 18:22–23
90. Isa:24:8–9; Jer:7:34, Jer:16:9, Jer:25:10,
91. Rev 18:23–24
92. Gen 3:6

things of the world. If someone loves the world, then love for the Father is not in him; because all the things of the world — the desires of the old nature, the desires of the eyes, and the pretensions of life — are not from the Father but from the world."[93]

Yochanan often prayed that the future generations would read and understand the power of the testimony he witnessed through the oracle he received on the island of Patmos as he heard the words, "They defeated him [the dragon] because of the Lamb's blood and because of the message of their witness. Even when facing death they did not cling to life."[94]As she ceases to exist, the influence Babylon wielded over the nations of the earth through her commerce and music suddenly comes to a stop.

> After these things, I heard what sounded like the roar of a huge crowd in heaven, shouting, "Halleluyah! The victory, the glory, the power of our God! For his judgments are true and just. He has judged the great whore who corrupted the earth with her whoring. He has taken vengeance on her who has the blood of his servants on her hands."[95]

As they see the judgement of the Great Whore, who quenched her thirst for glory and power with their blood, her victims rejoice. Yochanan is elated as he watches the end of the story. "There will be a happy ending for the saints of God!" he thinks to himself, "May HaShem give them the patience to hold on till the end!" They wait patiently for him, and he answers. They rely on his vindication and he avenges them. Their lives were lives of hard labor; when cursed they kept on blessing; when persecuted, they put up with it; when slandered, they continued their work![96] Oh, he was so proud of them, of all of them throughout the ages who, "through trusting, conquered kingdoms, worked righteousness, received what was promised, shut the mouths of lions, quenched the power of fire, escaped the edge of the sword, had their weakness turned to strength, grew mighty in battle and routed

93. 1 John 2:15–16
94. Rev 12:11
95. Rev 19:1–2
96. 1 Cor 4:12–13

foreign armies…underwent the trials of being mocked and whipped, then chained and imprisoned...stoned, sawed in two, murdered by the sword. No, the world was certainly not worthy of them!"[97]

And a second time they said, "Halleluyah! Her smoke goes up forever and ever!"[98]

The testimony of Babylon's judgement, of the sentence of her who persecuted HaShem's children will endure forever. It will stand as a perpetual testimony of HaShem's justice and vindication of his saints.

> The twenty-four elders and the four living beings fell down and worshipped God, sitting on the throne, and said, "Amen! Halleluyah!" A voice went out from the throne, saying, "Praise our God, all you his servants, you who fear him, small and great!"[99]

Yochanan is in awe as he watches the cherubim around HaShem's throne give glory to the Almighty for the judgment of the great whore.

97. Heb 11:33–38
98. Rev 19:3
99. Rev 19:4–5

CHAPTER 6
A UNION SET IN HEAVEN

- The Wedding Banquet
- The Bridegroom is Coming! The Bridegroom is Coming!
- The Messianic Age Fulfilled at Last
- Another Test for Humanity
- The Judge Gives the Final Sentence

The Wedding Banquet

The great enemy of HaShem's people through the ages has finally been annihilated. "Hopefully, she will not rise again," thinks Yochanan. His sigh of relief is interrupted by a great commotion, something he is familiar with from the ancient writings about the events at Mount Horeb.[1]

> Then I heard what sounded like the roar of a huge crowd, like the sound of rushing waters, like loud peals of thunder, saying, "Halleluyah! ADONAI, God of heaven's armies, has begun his reign! "Let us rejoice and be glad! Let us give him the glory! For the time has come for the wedding of the Lamb, and his Bride has prepared herself—fine linen, bright and clean has been given her to wear."[2]

The false bride, the whore and mother of all prostitutes, has received her due. Through the ages, she sought to depose the real bride, the mother of obedient and righteous Israel who is now called to receive her reward.

1. Exod 19;
2. Rev 19:6–8 ("Fine linen" means the righteous deeds of God's people.)

The wedding in Horeb is the most awesome event relating to HaShem intersecting with man on earth since the Garden of Eden. Yochanan remembers the faithful apostle who had recently written to the discouraged Israeli believers. As the Master had foretold, they had been chased out of the Temple and synagogues. They felt lost and hopeless, so one of the emissaries wrote them a letter encouraging and exhorting them to look at the end reward with courage. In his exhortation, the writer tells them,

> So, strengthen your drooping arms, and steady your tottering knees; and make a level path for your feet; so that what has been injured will not get wrenched out of joint but rather will be healed. Keep pursuing shalom with everyone and the holiness without which no one will see the Lord. See to it that no one misses out on God's grace, that no root of bitterness springing up causes trouble and thus contaminates many.... For you have not come to a tangible mountain, to an ignited fire, to darkness, to murk, to a whirlwind, to the sound of a shofar, and to a voice whose words made the hearers beg that no further message be given to them...and so terrifying was the sight that Moshe said, "I am quaking with dread." On the contrary, you have come to Mount Tziyon, that is, the city of the living God, heavenly Yerushalayim; to myriads of angels in festive assembly; to a community of the firstborn; to the mediator of a new covenant, Yeshua; and to the sprinkled blood that speaks better things than that of Hevel... Even then, his voice shook the earth; but now, he has made this promise: "One more time I will shake not only the earth, but heaven too!" And this phrase, "one more time," makes clear that the things shaken are removed, since they are created things, so that the things not shaken may remain. Therefore, since we have received an unshakeable Kingdom, let us have grace, through which we may offer service that will please God, with reverence and fear. For indeed, "Our God is a consuming fire!"[3]

If the revelation on Mount Horeb, the revelation orchestrated for the first redeemer, was so awesome, how much more awesome could the

3. Heb 12:12–29

revelation at Mount Zion, the revelation orchestrated for the second redeemer (of which the first redeemer is type) be!

Yochanan is again asked to write:

> The angel said to me, "Write: 'How blessed are those who have been invited to the wedding feast of the Lamb!'" Then he added, "These are God's very words."[4]

The invitations to the great wedding have been since days of old. For centuries, Israelites dreamed of the day they will recline for a meal with Abraham and the other patriarchs. Now, believers from not only Israel but from all nations will join them. What a party that will be! What a kiddush, prayer, that will be led by the Master, who will drink of the fruit of the vine for the first time since he drank with his disciples in Israel, many centuries before, on a special Passover night.[5]

Yochanan is awed at the realization that he has been hearing HaShem's very words.

> I fell at his feet to worship him; but he said, "Don't do that! I'm only a fellow-servant with you and your brothers who have the testimony of Yeshua. Worship God! For the testimony of Yeshua is the Spirit of prophecy."[6]

Yochanan realizes then that he hasn't been in communication with an angelic being, but with a departed believer, maybe one who had been martyred for the Name of Yeshua. This is one who, unlike the angels, understands in a personal way what the messianic congregations are going through. He can, therefore, appreciate the encouragement and blessing of this message.

Deeply entrenched in the vision, Yochanan watches as history repeats itself. As in the days of the destruction of the Temple, the armies of the nations surround Jerusalem again. There is a great turmoil. The city seems lost. He watches as the east side of the city appears to him, the Mount of Olives, where he spent many memorable

4. Rev 19:9
5. Mt 26:29
6. Rev 19:10

moments with the Master and the other disciples. The earth shakes in a colossal earthquake, an earthquake so strong, that the one in the days of Uzziah, the king of Judah, pales in comparison.[7] The mountain cracks open east to west, carving out a sizable valley. Half of the mountain is moved toward the north, and half of it toward the south.[8]

The Bridegroom is Coming! The Bridegroom is Coming!

> Next I saw heaven opened, and there before me was a white horse. Sitting on it was the one called Faithful and True, and it is in righteousness that he passes judgment and goes to battle.[9]

Yom Kippur has not passed yet. The heavens are still opened to receive the prayers of the believers; to evaluate their deeds; to take stock of their lives for the books.[10] The whore is no more, and the believers have been called to their reward. But this year, Yom Kippur will be very different. As the repenting prayers of the saints ascend to heaven, they are answered by the appearing redeemer.

Yochanan can't believe his eyes: A formidable white horse accompanied by an awe-inspiring rider. This is not like the one he saw earlier when the Master broke the first seal of the scroll in HaShem's hand.[11] This is not the false god of this earth trying to imitate the peace of the Kingdom of God. This is not a satanically inspired puppet emperor bringing peace and plenty to a select elite supported by the under-privileged poor masses of the world. This is not the one who will build his empire on the blood of HaShem's saints. This is the

7. Amos 1:1; Zech 14:5

8. Zech 14:1–15

9. Rev 19:11

10. Dan 7:10 According to the Talmud, on Rosh Hashanah we are inscribed in one of three books: the book of life, death and in-between Those of us who have been saintly are automatically written in the book of life, while those of us who have been evil are penned in the book of death. The rest are given ten days, known as "Days of Awe," to set our lives on the correct path.

11. Rev 6:1–2

real redeemer. The long-awaited Prince of Peace, the one prophesied by Moses and all the prophets, the king of Israel long-awaited by the people of God. He is the one who comes to bring vengeance and redemption upon all those who since the days of Abel, the sons of Adam have been persecuted and killed for righteousness' sake. He is the one who truly brings a fair chance at peace, plenty, liberty, and justice for all, not just for a select few at the cost of others.

> His eyes were like a fiery flame, and on his head were many royal crowns. And he had a name written which no one knew but himself.[12]

"There is no mistaking this time," thinks Yochanan, when he sees the same fiery eyes that he saw when his Master appeared to him at the beginning of the vision.[13]

> He was wearing a robe that had been soaked in blood, and the name by which he is called is, "THE WORD OF GOD."[14]

How glad Yochanan was for the times he spent studying the words of the prophet, especially those of the messianic visions Isaiah received. How precious to him are the words of the ancient prophet who, in an Abrahamic vision, saw the Messiah coming in a garment dipped in blood.[15] Yes, the brethren were persecuted. Yes, for the community of believers, the waiting for the return of the Master felt like a woman being in excruciating, never-ending labor. But oh, what a joy; oh, what fruit came because of their suffering; oh, what a conclusion. Now they understand Isaiah who once saw HaShem, "giving them garlands instead of ashes, the oil of gladness instead of mourning, a cloak of praise instead of a heavy spirit, so that they will be called oaks of righteousness planted by ADONAI, in which he takes pride."[16]

The Master himself, he who paved the way of discipleship by introducing them to persecution for righteousness' sake and to

12. Rev 19:12
13. Rev 1:14
14. Rev 19:13
15. Isa 63:1
16. Isa 61:3

crucifixion, was coming back in his resurrected body to take revenge on his and their enemies. And he was not alone.

> The armies of heaven, clothed in fine linen, white and pure, were following him on white horses.[17]

In those days, all those who would not bow the knee to the Roman idolatrous laws would be severely punished. Both Jews and Gentiles who disobeyed were considered criminals. Yochanan is proud of those faithful disciples who endured persecution without flinching. He remembers what the Master told him one time, "For if someone is ashamed of me and of what I say in this adulterous and sinful generation, the Son of Man also will be ashamed of him when he comes in his Father's glory with the holy angels."[18] Now, he is coming in his glory with the holy angels. What a beautiful sight. Hope was never in vain.

> And out of his mouth comes a sharp sword with which to strike down nations—"He will rule them with a staff of iron."[19]

"That sword again, just as I saw in the beginning," Yochanan thinks of his dear colleague, Paul, now resting at Abraham's side[20] waiting for the final resurrection, who taught about that "sword" as an analogy to the word of God itself.[21]

> It is he who treads the winepress from which flows the wine of the furious rage of ADONAI, God of heaven's armies.[22]

In this fall season, the grape harvest is drawing to its end. There will be wine for the Sukkot festivities. What a time for our Master to come and apply his vengeance on his enemies like those who crush the grapes with their feet.

---

17. Rev 19:14
18. Mar 8:38
19. Rev 19:15
20. Lu 16:22
21. Eph 6:17
22. Rev 19:15

> And on his robe and on his thigh he has a name written: KING OF KINGS AND LORD OF LORDS.[23]

King Cyrus of Persia who allowed the Jerusalem Temple to be rebuilt liked to bear the title of "king of kings." Though he allowed the rebuilding of Jerusalem and the return of the captives, he kept control over Israel, thus Israel learned that there is a price to pay. Yet, the true King of Kings, who will accomplish the construction of the third Temple, comes to provide true freedom and true deliverance to his people.

> Then I saw an angel standing in the sun, and he cried out in a loud voice to all the birds that fly about in mid-heaven, "Come, gather together for the great feast God is giving, to eat the flesh of kings, the flesh of generals, the flesh of important men, the flesh of horses and their riders and the flesh of all kinds of people, free and slave, small and great!"[24]

Vultures have this sixth sense which tells them when their prey is about to succumb. They ride on the wings of the wind in an eerie circular dance and patiently wait. Our vulture, the one Yochanan has seen circling the sky from early on in the vision, seemed to have a premonition that a great holocaust was imminent. He is right; an angel calls for all the scavenger birds of the earth.

> I saw the beast and the kings of the earth and their armies gathered together to do battle with the rider of the horse and his army.[25]

That famous valley where Yochanan used to dream when he was a child is about to become the theater of the battle of all battles: the true battle for freedom.

> But the beast was taken captive, and with it the false prophet who, in its presence, had done the miracles which he had used to deceive those who had received the mark of the beast and those who had

23. Rev 19:16
24. Rev 19:17–18
25. Rev 19:19

> worshipped his image. The beast and the false prophet were both thrown alive into the lake of fire that burns with sulfur.[26]

As he violently overcame Pharaoh's pride and gently led Israel to the wedding canopy of Mount Horeb; as he victoriously overthrew the blasphemous whore to receive his holy bride at his table; he now overcomes the realm of the beast, its false prophet, and all those who swore them allegiance. He who won the battle in the desert; he who stayed strong in Gethsemane; he who gave his life at Golgotha now captures his enemy in the Valley of Armageddon. The Kingdom, the prophet, and all those associated with them through the evil mark on their hand and forehead are sent to be consumed in the lake of fire.

As Pharaoh threw the males of Israel in the Red Sea, those cosmic persecutors of the people of God are now thrown in the red fiery flames of HaShem's judgment. As he sees the people who received the mark of the beast, the antithesis to the Jewish tefillins on their hands and foreheads, go to the lake of fire, Yochanan remembers the word of his Master, "If your right eye makes you sin, gouge it out and throw it away! Better that you should lose one part of you than have your whole body thrown into Gei-Hinnom. And if your right hand makes you sin, cut it off and throw it away! Better that you should lose one part of you than have your whole body thrown into Gei-Hinnom."[27]

> The rest were killed with the sword that goes out of the mouth of the rider on the horse, and all the birds gorged themselves on their flesh.[28]

Yochanan contemplates the words of his Master. He remembers him teaching that these times will be like the days of the great flood. Those protected for a season returned after the wrath of God was poured upon

26. Rev 19:20
27. Mt 5:29-30
28. Rev 19:21

the earth, after the birds did the great clean up, satisfying themselves from the flesh of those who were left behind.[29]

The Messianic Age Fulfilled; At Last!

> Next I saw an angel coming down from heaven, who had the key to the Abyss and a great chain in his hand.[30]

The whore was no more. The kingdom of the beast and the false prophet were sent to the lake of fire. These were but pawns, tools in the hands of HaSatan, the Serpent, who since the days of Adam sought to steal mankind's loyalty.

> He seized the dragon, that ancient serpent, who is the Devil and Satan [the Adversary] and chained him up for a thousand years. He threw him into the Abyss, locked it and sealed it over him; so that he could not deceive the nations any more until the thousand years were over. After that, he has to be set free for a little while.[31]

HaSatan who has deceived the world into disobedience since the days of Eve is now thrown in the Abyss opened by the angel.[32]There he will reside, and with him the evil inclination of mankind. With the accuser[33] defeated, the heavenly court is now in order. The defense asks the accused, "Where are they? Has no one condemned you?" To which the repentant soul answers, "No one, sir." Yeshua then replies, "Neither do I condemn you. Now go, and don't sin anymore."[34] Their sins are not deleted; they are simply paid for.

> Then I saw thrones, and those seated on them received authority to judge. And I saw the souls of those who had been beheaded for testifying about Yeshua and proclaiming the Word of God, also

29. Mat 24:28; 37
30. Rev 20:1
31. Rev 20:2–3
32. Rev 9
33. Rev 12:10
34. Jn 8:10–11

> those who had not worshipped the beast or its image and had not received the mark on their foreheads and on their hands. They came to life and ruled with the Messiah for a thousand years.[35/36]

Finally, the king, or rather, the King of Kings, comes to occupy the Jerusalem throne that belonged to him since the day of creation. How many times did Yochanan envision that glorious scene as he remembered the Daniel oracles[37] and heard his Master teach about it?[38]All the martyrs of all the ages sit as judges. Who else could have enough of a sense of justice but those who have been the victims of the cruel injustice of the government of man? The poor, the persecuted, the widow, she who suffered under a wicked husband; peoples and nations will come to them with their grief. Like Solomon of old, Yeshua and his saints will apply righteous judgments. They will not judge with the seeing of the eyes or with the hearing of the ears. They will administer true justice; a justice where evil is punished, righteousness rewarded, and victims vindicated through proper retribution.[39] The poor will be considered. The broken-hearted will be healed. The captives will be made free and those who walk in darkness will see the light in that favorable year of Yeshua. All the unaddressed injustice committed since the day of Abel's murder will be visited in that day of vengeance of our Master and Redeemer, when he comes to comfort all that mourn.[40] All wrongs will be righted. These will be the days when the Messiah's supernal Torah will be the rule of Law. These will be the days when finally, the renewed covenant prophecies that Jeremiah spoke of will be fulfilled. Finally, the words the Master taught his disciple on the mountain come alive to Yochanan.[41]

35. Babylonian Talmud Chapter 11 tractate Sanhedrin
36. Rev 20:4
37. Dan 7:9
38. Mt 19:28
39. Isa 11
40. Isa 61:1–2
41. Mt 5:1–12

> (The rest of the dead did not come to life until the thousand years were over.) This is the first resurrection.[42]

Yochanan watches the whole plan unfold, scene by scene. He understands what he has been preparing for every year during the season of Yom Kippur and the feast of Sukkot. The sages had predicted it, that the war to end all wars for the establishment of the Kingdom of God on earth and the resurrection would happen during the fall feasts at the time of Sukkot.

> Blessed and holy is anyone who has a part in the first resurrection; over him the second death has no power. On the contrary, they will be cohanim of God and of the Messiah, and they will rule with him for the thousand years.[43]

The martyrs, those who "had been beheaded for testifying about Yeshua and proclaiming the Word of God, also those who had not worshipped the beast or its image and had not received the mark on their foreheads and on their hands,"[44] rule and judge the masses of the people on earth with the Messiah. During that time, those who sold themselves to the Adversary of all righteousness stay in a dormant state like that of the rich man in the parable of Lazarus and the Rich Man.[45]

For a thousand years, the world knows peace, righteousness, beauty, fairness, justice, and abundance above measure. The world can see, feel, and benefit from a universe run under the laws of Yeshua's Torah. Faith that is, the confidence of what we hope for, and the conviction of what we do not see,[46] is obsolete, because every eye can see the Son.[47] Yochanan, understands the trials of those who have not had this privilege. It is more difficult to believe having not seen, but yet, more blessed.[48] But is the question of belief and obedience a matter of evidence? Did the world rebel because they had no proof?

42. Rev 20:5
43. Rev 20:6
44. Rev 20:4
45. Lu 16
46. Heb 11
47. Rev 1:7
48. Jn 20:29

Another Test For Humanity

> When the thousand years are over, the Adversary will be set free from his prison and will go out to deceive the nations in the four quarters of the earth, Gog and Magog, to gather them for the battle. Their number is countless as the sand on the seashore;[49]

To his great disappointment, Yochanan sees, again, a repeat of history. When given a choice, even in the face of the evidence of the glory of the Kingdom of God on earth, man chooses to rebel. From the times of the beauty of the Garden of Eden until now, the same story seems to curse humanity. The valley of his tender youth, this valley that had flourished during that era of peace, becomes again the theater of war.

> And they came up over the breadth of the Land and surrounded the camp of God's people and the city he loves. But fire came down from heaven and consumed them.[50]

Jerusalem, which finally lived up to its name, is again surrounded by armies. As the Son came 1,000 years before, now the Father comes in his fury to execute judgment against those who would persecute his children.

> The Adversary who had deceived them was hurled into the lake of fire and sulfur, where the beast and the false prophet were; and they will be tormented day and night forever and ever.[51]

Yochanan lets out a sigh of relief as he sees HaSatan, whom HaShem used in order to test humanity, now united with the beast and the false prophet in the lake of fire. Never again will he roam the earth accusing them before HaShem. Never again will he have the power to deceive men. Never again will his influence be allowed.

---

49. Rev 20:7–8
50. Rev 20:9
51. Rev 20:10

The Judge Gives the Final Sentence

> Next I saw a great white throne and the One sitting on it. Earth and heaven fled from his presence, and no place was found for them.[52]

Yochanan can hardly contain a scream of awe as he watches. The earth and the skies are so contaminated by sinful man that they cannot even stand before their Almighty Creator. Like Adam in the garden after he disobeyed couldn't find anywhere to hide, the universe is also scrambling to hide before the presence of the Presence. For millennia, creation, frustrated by those who pollute it, waits eagerly for this moment. Until now, it has been groaning as with the pains of childbirth, waiting to deliver HaShem's Kingdom on earth.[53]

> And I saw the dead, both great and small, standing in front of the throne. Books were opened; and another book was opened, the Book of Life; and the dead were judged from what was written in the books, according to what they had done.[54]

The great judgment has come. Those who have not changed their ways and repented; those who clung to the evil inclination; those who received the mark of the kingdom of the beast and who are waiting dormant now rise to face the Day of Anger, when HaShem's righteous judgment is revealed; when he pays back each one according to his deeds.[55] Yochanan remembers that day in Jerusalem during Passover. The Master healed an invalid who, for 38 years, had hoped for healing by plunging in the Bethesda pool as an angel came to stir the waters. That man didn't know that even the angels feared him who was talking to him. It was such a magnificent healing. The man was so happy. On that day, Yeshua talked about the authority that HaShem gave him. He even said that "the time is coming when all who are in the grave will hear

52. Rev 20:11
53. Rom 8:19-22
54. Rev 20:12
55. Rom 2:5-6

his voice and come out — those who have done good to a resurrection of life, and those who have done evil to a resurrection of judgment."[56]

> The sea gave up the dead in it; and Death and Sh'ol gave up the dead in them; and they were judged, each according to what he had done.[57]

Yochanan thinks of the time when the daughters of man had relations with the sons of God.[58]Enoch, the first scribe wrote in his book that as a punishment, these women were sent to be sirens, spirits in the sea.[59]Death and Sh'ol, which held many who failed to repent of their ungodliness during their lifetime, were also to come to face judgment. Now, the souls under the altar rejoice and see firsthand the punishment of those who used and abused them.[60]

> Then Death and Sh'ol were hurled into the lake of fire. This is the second death — the lake of fire.[61]

That place of holding where unrepentant souls wait for their judgment becomes obsolete. It is now thrown in the lake of fire to be purified. Death is finally abolished and swallowed up in victory.[62]

> Anyone whose name was not found written in the Book of Life was hurled into the lake of fire.[63]

Yochanan realizes that this is not the yearly fall festival rehearsal; it is the real thing. There will not be another chance.

---

56. Jn 5:28
57. Rev 20:13
58. Gen 6:1-4
59. Book of Enoch chapter 19. And Uriel said to me: "Here shall stand the angels who have connected themselves with women, and their spirits assuming many different forms are defiling mankind and shall lead them astray into sacrificing to demons [as gods], (here shall they stand) till [the day of] the great judgement in which they shall be judged till they are made an end of.. And the women also of the angels who went astray shall become sirens." And I, Enoch, alone saw the vision, the ends of all things: and no man shall see as I have seen.
60. Rev 6:9-11
61. Rev 20:14
62. 2 Tim 1:10; 1 Cor 15:54
63. Rev 20:15

CHAPTER 7
THE GLORY OF THE BRIDE

- The Bride is Coming, the Bride is Coming!
- The Mountain of the City of HaShem
- The Tribes in the Desert and Earthly Jerusalem Foreshadow the Bride
- Epilogue

The Bride is Coming! The Bride is Coming!

Yom Kippur is past. The gavel has fallen. The books are closed. The heavens have closed again. The court is no longer in session. Now comes the time of Tabernacles, when the children of Israel remember their time with Moses in the desert by building booths. While prisoner in the Isle of Patmos, Yochanan may not have been able to build himself one as he has so often done in Jerusalem in the company of the other disciples. Suddenly, the whole of creation begins again in front of Yochanan.

> Then I saw a new heaven and a new earth, for the old heaven and the old earth had passed away, and the sea was no longer there.[1]

Yochanan remembers the words of the prophet Isaiah who spoke of this restoration of heaven and earth.[2] The disciple watches as the old heaven and the old earth undergo a purifying rebirth process. He also remembers the words of the wise apostle Paul, who was sometimes hard to understand, as he gave hope to his disciples.[3] Speaking to them

1. Rev 21:1
2. Isa 65:17
3. 2 Peter 3:14–16

of the renewal of the earth, he said, "man has subjected creation to sin, for the creation was made subject to frustration — not willingly, but because of the one who subjected it. But it was given a reliable hope that it too would be set free from its bondage to decay and would enjoy the freedom accompanying the glory that God's children will have."[4] Yes, as man was subjected to sin, he subjected the creation to frustration. But as HaShem renews man, he also renews the creation that is the signature of his glory.

The renewed will be freed from the Abyss of the great sea that bordered Israel to the west. The tanin, the sea monster which inhabited it, will have no more places to hide.

> Also I saw the holy city, New Yerushalayim, coming down out of heaven from God, prepared like a bride beautifully dressed for her husband.[5]

First perceived by Abraham[6], conquered and established by King David, destroyed by Nebuchadnezzar, rebuilt after the Babylonian captivity, improved by Herod, and now destroyed by the Romans, Jerusalem had seen its share of trouble and sorrow. The earthly city of peace had undergone so many battles, conquests, and wars, that Yochanan cannot imagine that it could withstand anymore. It flourished during the time of Solomon, and Yochanan saw its glory in the time of the reign of Yeshua on earth, but now it is destroyed again in that great battle of Gog and Magog. It always seems that it cannot rise without falling. Never in his wildest imagination would he have dreamed he'd set his eyes on the heavenly Jerusalem spoken of by Isaiah.[7] Heaven and earth had been purified first of their satanic inhabitants, then of their death and decay and finally renewed to be able to receive the Jerusalem from above. The emotional disciple remembers how he spent his life with his brothers and sisters, telling people to die to

4. Rom 8:20–21
5. Rev 21:2
6. Gen 22:4: Abraham saw "The Place," *HaKom* in Hebrew ,המקום refers to the fact that he saw the future city of Jerusalem that will be built there. The author of Hebrews confirms this: For he [Abraham] was looking forward to the city with permanent foundations, of which the architect and builder is God. Heb 11:10
7. Isa 65:17;19

their old selves so that they will be renewed as fit tabernacles for the presence of HaShem's Spirit within them. Now he understands the microcosm, the purpose of it all. Now he understands why he had to write the letters to the congregations. The Kingdom is truly at hand and they need to be fit vessels. Eyes have truly not seen, and ear truly not heard what HaShem has prepared for all those who love him.[8]

Yochanan can hardly keep the story from flooding in his mind.

From the days of Adam and Eve, HaShem's people have waited for the renewal of the lost heaven on earth, when the divine presence of God lived and freely roamed the earth in mankind's company.[9] In the days of Noah, the earth had become filled with Cain-like violence, influenced by the fallen angels,[10] and then underwent a massive universal immersion rebirth. Having set certain parameters of conduct with humanity through Noah's family, HaShem established a relationship covenant with a promise to never destroy the earth through water.[11]

Little by little, HaShem was bringing mankind into an awareness of his Kingdom. It is when he appeared in glory to Moses that not only the children of Israel, but also the whole world learned more fully of the ways of the Kingdom. As David conquered the city of Salem in the land of Canaan, David saw the city where HaShem would set his Name. As he desired to build a more glorious tabernacle for his God, the great plan was revealed to him through Nathan, the faithful prophet. Nathan spoke of a descendant of David who would be called son of HaShem his father, and who will establish a Kingdom which will last forever[12].

Since that time, people have understood that the Messiah, begotten by the God who created heaven and earth, would come and rule the world from Jerusalem. That is why the Maccabean kings were never accepted, why Herod was not a legitimate king of the Jews, since only a descendant of David can inherit the throne of Jerusalem. Anyone else is an imposter of the coming Messiah. This Messiah, who would

8. Isa 64:4
9. Gen 3:8
10. Gen 6:1–7
11. Gen 9:1–17
12. 2 Sam 7:1–17

establish Jerusalem as the capital of a world under the rule of Torah, has since been the expectation of Israel.

The day of his coming will be the day of the great resurrection; a resurrection when the perishable is swallowed and replaced by the eternal.[13] As citizens of the Kingdom, we will don the imperishable, non-decaying robe of the Kingdom, and have the same type of bodies Adam and Eve had before sin stripped them of their heavenly attributes. A body like the Master's when he resurrected. [14]

Yochanan remembers his teacher, the Immerser, pleading to everyone to repent and clean up their lives in expectation that the Messiah's time was at hand. He remembers going also with the Master teaching in synagogues that the time of the Kingdom was at hand.[15] What a beautiful time of expectation it was! Everybody expected the Master to raise an army, drive the Romans out, and sit on the throne of Jerusalem, establishing the Kingdom of Heaven on earth. He even taught others to pray for it in daily prayers, May your Kingdom come, your will be done on earth as in heaven.[16] But though he initiated the messianic era, setting the time "at hand," he also injected the notion of a Kingdom that needed more time to find its establishment on earth. Earth was not ready yet. He compared the Kingdom to a mustard seed planted in the ground that needed time to grow before all the birds of the earth came to find refuge under it. He also spoke of the Kingdom like leaven needing time to raise a batch of dough.[17]

Even in the days of Yochanan, people were impatient about the never-coming Kingdom. His faithful friend, Kefa, now sleeping with his fathers, tried to help believers around him to understand that the reason for the needed time is to give a chance to everyone. He taught that we cannot be selfish and hope for it to come right now just because we have our citizenship in it. HaShem did not have just Israel in mind, but the world![18]

13. 1 Cor 15:50–58
14. Lu 24:39
15. Mt 4:23
16. Mt 6:10
17. Mt 13:31–33
18. 2 Pet 3:1–9

Yochanan, who was present at the Jerusalem council that decided to allow Gentiles into the covenant of Israel through the sole acceptance of discipleship capped with a few other rules, remembers James quoting the words of Amos the prophet, "After this, I will return; and I will rebuild the fallen tent of David. I will rebuild its ruins, I will restore it, so that the rest of mankind may seek the Lord, that is, all the Goyim who have been called by my name," (Act 15:16-17)

He also undertood better Isaiah's words of prophecy concerning the gathering of the exiles of Israel."[19]

Yochanan understands the long summer months between the spring and fall feasts as this time of waiting, and waiting, and waiting. He has been part of the effort to teach people in other countries about citizenship in the coming Kingdom of Heaven on earth. How long will it be until when Yeshua will actually reign in Jerusalem in the company of his disciples and followers? How long will it be until the earth is compliant enough, pure enough, and clean enough to become the home of the real Tabernacle in the heavenlies, of New Jerusalem? In this vision on the Isle of Patmos, Yochanan sees what started as a promise to the fathers and the prophets as a soon-coming reality.

> I heard a loud voice from the throne say, "See! God's Sh'khinah is with mankind, and he will live with them. They will be his people, and he himself, God-with-them, will be their God.[20]

The voice of the Master who now sits on the throne of glory his Father gave him points Yochanan to the continuing vision. Given an opportunity to look at HaShem's Shekinah, he ponders the ancient texts. Animated by the promise that HaShem would live among the people of Israel, Moses built a tabernacle.[21] This tabernacle was to be a replica of the original that Moses had seen on the mountain. Yochanan feels so honored to also be given a glimpse of what the future holds. He can hardly wait to share these words of hope with the distressed disciples that are left in Israel, as well as those of the congregations in Asia Minor. He knows that this is what they need to find the hope

19. Isa 56:8
20. Rev 21:3
21. Exod 25:8

to hold on to. He realizes also that the generations of both Jewish and Gentile disciples to come will need to know of this vision and of all these words if they are to hold on to the end, however long that may be, until the harvest of humanity is reaped.

> He will wipe away every tear from their eyes. There will no longer be any death; and there will no longer be any mourning, crying or pain; because the old order has passed away. Then the One sitting on the throne said, "Look! I am making everything new!" Also he said, "Write, these words are true and trustworthy![22]

Already in the days of Isaiah, HaShem desired to comfort his people with a vision of what is to come. Yochanan knows the tears shed by the disciples under the imperial persecutions, but he is also aware of the tears of the world around him. Tribes, ethnic groups, and whole nations have suffered throughout the centuries. No vial can hold the tears shed on the earth due to man's injustice and cruelty. The widow, the orphan, the poor, the used and abused, the oppressed and the persecuted, have also shed many tears. No receptacle is big enough to receive the sorrow, weeping, and suffering endured by a world devoid of HaShem's laws. In the place of purity, death was brought to the earth through disobedience, death which is the payment for our sins[23]of pride, lust, greed, and rebellion, becomes obsolete.

But mourning is replaced by feasting. It is with great joy and anticipation that Yochanan writes these words that he knows are essential to the encouragement and patience of his brothers and sisters in the diaspora. The voice of the Master continues thundering.

> And he said to me, "It is done! I am the Aleph א and the Tav ת the Beginning and the End. To anyone who is thirsty I myself will give water free of charge from the Fountain of Life."[24]

Oh yes; he is the "Aleph." He is the beginning of HaShem's creation,[25] and the establishment of his kingship over the earth is the ultimate

22. Rev 21:4–5
23. Rom 3:23
24. Rev 21:6
25. Prov 8:22–30

fulfillment of HaShem's purpose. Yochanan remembers that little midrash he was taught in school. That in HaShem are the beginning and the end, the aleph and the tav, the first and last letters of the Hebrew alphabet. When all the variant letters are counted, mem is the middle letter, which when placed between the first and last, forms the word "*emet* (truth) אמת." As he hears these words from the throne, Yochanan remembers his Master saying, "I am … the truth אנכי … האמת."[26]

Many thirst for the justice and righteousness of the HaShem's Kingdom. As he promised a few decades before,[27] the Messiah offered to fill those who put their trust in him. He calls, "All you who are thirsty, come to the water! You without money, come, buy, and eat! Yes, come! Buy wine and milk without money — it's free!" He also reminds people not work for what does not satisfy. "Why spend money for what isn't food, your wages for what doesn't satisfy? Listen carefully to me, and you will eat well, you will enjoy the fat of the land.[28]

> He who wins the victory will receive these things, and I will be his God, and he will be my son.[29]

Now Yochanan understands what it is to "win the victory." The disciples must stay strong. They must not give in to the deception and lies of the imposter messiah. They must not let their fleshly appetites push them toward compromise for the sake of a little meat, a little comfort, a little recognition. This had been Eve's problem, as Yochanan often taught: "The desires of the old nature, the desires of the eyes, and the pretensions of life —which are not from the Father but from the world."[30] The Master had given them the antidote against compromise: the Lamb's blood, the message of their witness, and

26. Jn 14:6
27. Mt 5:6
28. Isa 55:1–2; Jn 6:27
29. Rev 21:7
30. 1 John 2:16

when facing death, not to cling to life.[31] As this world passes away, along with its desires, whoever does God's will remains forever.[32]

> But as for the cowardly, the untrustworthy, the vile, the murderers, the sexually immoral, those involved with the occult and with drugs, idol-worshippers, and all liars — their destiny is the lake burning with fire and sulfur, the second death.[33]

Yochanan had seen many missing the mark of their calling because of cowardice caused by ambivalence due to fear. But the Master was very clear: we cannot serve two masters. We cannot serve HaShem and money.[34] For the timid, the liar, the wicked, the slaughterer of the innocent, and for all those who without repentance indulged their flesh and spirit in those things which HaShem abhors, this was the end.

The Mountain of The City of Hashem

> One of the seven angels having the seven bowls full of the seven last plagues approached me and said, "Come! I will show you the Bride, the Wife of the Lamb." He carried me off in the Spirit to the top of a great, high mountain and showed me the holy city, Yerushalayim, coming down out of heaven from God.[35]

Yochanan cannot believe his eyes. Is this really the Jerusalem from above? Is this the city Abraham, the patriarchs, and the prophets saw in their visions and in their dreams? Is this, "the city with permanent foundations, of which the architect and builder is God?"[36] Is this what we have been waiting for all along?

> It had the Sh'khinah of God, so that its brilliance was like that of a priceless jewel, like a crystal-clear diamond.[37]

31. Rev 12:11
32. 1 John 2:17
33. Rev 21:8
34. Mt 6:24
35. Rev 21:9–10
36. Heb 11:10
37. Rev 21:11

The whole mountain shone from within.[38] How could he, like Moses, been able to behold the Shekinah of God? Neither the most beautiful, nor the richest palace on earth, could compete with the beauty of HaShem's city.

> It had a great, high wall with twelve gates; at the gates were twelve angels; and inscribed on the gates were the names of the twelve tribes of Isra'el.[39]

Now Yochanan understands the plan. He understands the saga which contributed to the building of Jacob's family. He understands the adoption of Ephraim and Manasseh by Jacob their grandfather. He understands why HaShem's Torah provided for the preservation of the tribes and of their inheritance. He understands the yearly festivals, the practice of Jubilees. Everything becomes clear now as he contemplates the role Israel as a federation of tribes is to play in the grand scheme of things.

Since the time it was built, the Temple in Jerusalem was the place to where Israel and the nations turned their prayers. It was the place where the whole world came in the presence of HaShem Again, these very tribes of the families of Israel become the gates, humanity's entrance points to the great, heavenly tabernacle.

> There were three gates to the east, three gates to the north, three gates to the south and three gates to the west.[40]

It is no wonder that from the very beginning, HaSatan tried to conquer, subjugate, annihilate, and destroy Israel. He knew that salvation came through Israel.[41] Destroying the descendants of the family of Jacob, he would destroy the first fruit of humanity's redemption,[42] but also the gates by which the redeemed enters the heavenly tabernacle. He tried so hard. He even had the gall to try to deceive Yeshua.

So much more makes sense. Yochanan can hardly contain his emotions. As a child, he had learned so much about the forefathers

38. Isa 2:2–3; 11:9
39. Rev 21:12
40. Rev 21:13
41. Jn 4:22
42. Rev 14:1–5

in the desert coming out of Egypt, traveling and following the cloud towards the Promised Land. Remembering the events of Balak and Balaam,[43] he and his friends often played "Moses and the tribes of Israel in the desert." They would reconstruct the position of the tribes around the holy ark, surrounded by the Levitical families and a friend who played Balaam would shout, "How lovely are your tents, Ya`akov; your encampments, Isra'el!"[44] Never had he imagined that the positions of the tribes mirrored the position of the gates of HaShem's heavenly tabernacle.

> The wall of the city was built on twelve foundation-stones, and on these were the twelve names of the twelve emissaries of the Lamb.[45]

The nascent messianic movement in Yochanan's days was rife with doctrinal divisions, cultural conflicts, as well as suffering intense persecutions at the hand of the Romans, and that of other Jews. All the disciples except Judas had died martyr's deaths. Yochanan was the last one alive. What a joy he must have felt; what a surprise it must have been when he saw his name and that of his friends on the foundation of the Holy City. In spite of all HaSatan throws at them, their lives and deaths eventually become the foundation upon which this heavenly New Jerusalem is built. Let him come with his prejudice, accusations, divisions, and temptations. Whether we stay alive, or he succeeds in killing us, HaSatan cannot prevail. Hope is therefore in order.

> The angel speaking with me had a gold measuring-rod with which to measure the city, its gates and its wall.[46]

Yochanan had previously seen an angel measuring the Temple in Jerusalem just prior to the time when his dear Master returns. Now this angel, who had also carried out the cleansing judgments on the earth, was to measure the heavenly city. "Didn't he already know its worth? Is it just to show me?" Yochanan wondered. As Yochanan noticed the gold measuring-rod, he remembered his friend Paul's words: "For

43. Num 22–24
44. Num 24:5
45. Rev 21:14
46. Rev 21:15

no one can lay any foundation other than the one already laid, which is Yeshua the Messiah. Some will use gold, silver or precious stones in building on this foundation; while others will use wood, grass or straw. But each one's work will be shown for what it is; the Day will disclose it, because it will be revealed by fire — the fire will test the quality of each one's work." [47] The angel measures the city against his gold-standard measuring rod.

The Tribes in the Desert and Earthly Jerusalem Foreshadow the Bride

> The city is laid out in a square, its length equal to its width. With his rod he measured the city at 1,500 miles, with length, width and height the same. He measured its wall at 216 feet by human standards of measurement, which the angel was using.[48]

As a giant Mount Horeb, the city lies square on the earth. At the magnificent sight, Yochanan concurs with the dear apostle who tried to impress upon the Israeli congregations the superior magnitude of the renewed covenant compared to that of Mount Horeb. when Hhe said, "For you have not come to a tangible mountain…On the contrary, you have come to Mount Tziyon, that is, the city of the living God, heavenly Yerushalayim; to myriads of angels in festive assembly; to a community of the firstborn whose names have been recorded in heaven; to a Judge who is God of everyone; to spirits of righteous people who have been brought to the goal; to the mediator of a new covenant, Yeshua; and to the sprinkled blood that speaks better things than that of Hevel."[49]

> The wall was made of diamond and the city of pure gold resembling pure glass. The foundations of the city wall were decorated with all kinds of precious stones — the first foundation stone was diamond, the second sapphire, the third chalcedony, the fourth emerald, the fifth sardonyx, the sixth carnelian, the seventh chrysolite, the eighth

47. 1 Cor 3:11-13
48. Rev 21: 16–17
49. Heb 12;18–24

> beryl, the ninth topaz, the tenth chrysoprase, the eleventh turquoise and the twelfth amethyst. The twelve gates were twelve pearls, with each gate made of a single pearl. The city's main street was pure gold, transparent as glass.[50]

Yochanan cries as he sees the city lying on the earth. Its square shape and multi-stoned foundation reminds him of Aaron's breastplate. Each precious stone in Aaron's breastplate stood for a tribe. The first high-priest of Israel used to wear it on his chest, near his heart, thus telling us how HaShem kept Israel and all its tribes close to his heart. Yochanan realizes that unknown to us all, Aaron was also showing us a part of the heavenly Jerusalem.

> I saw no Temple in the city, for ADONAI, God of heaven's armies, is its Temple, as is the Lamb.[51]

Though Yochanan would miss the beautiful Temple's liturgy, the singing of the elders of Israel praying to HaShem, the sound of the teachers instructing their disciples in the ways of the Torah, he knew that the Temple was only a gate to the presence of the Almighty God. He remembers the promise that one day, ."..all will know me [HaShem], from the least of them to the greatest; because I will forgive their wickedness and remember their sins no more." [52]

> The city has no need for the sun or the moon to shine on it, because God's Sh'khinah gives it light, and its lamp is the Lamb. The nations will walk by its light, and the kings of the earth will bring their splendor into it.[53]

As it was on the first four days of creation, before even the heavenly bodies were fashioned by the Almighty, humanity again walks in the primordial light, the light of the Lamb that showed its presence on the first day. As it was in the days of King Solomon, nations come to learn at HaShem's mountain, to walk by its light and learn wisdom from the Torah.

50. Rev 21:18–21
51. Rev 21:22
52. Jer 31:32–34
53. Rev 21: 23–24

> Its gates will never close, they stay open all day because night will not exist there, and the honor and splendor of the nations will be brought into it.[54]

Yochanan cannot retain his emotions as the vision before him brings to life the precious words from the prophet Isaiah: Your gates will always be open, they will not be shut by day or by night, so that people can bring you the wealth of nations, with their kings led in procession. [55]

> Nothing impure may enter it, nor anyone who does shameful things or lies; the only ones who may enter are those whose names are written in the Lamb's Book of Life.[56]

There are pools around the temple for people to immerse before entering it. Yochanan used them often with his friends. These pools saw the immersion of those who were added to the congregation on the first Shavuot after the resurrection of the Master, as well as of many others who came to identify Yeshua as the Messiah of Israel.[57] Nothing tamei/impure could enter in the Temple, but technically, it was practically impossible to keep it all pure/tahor. Some may lie about themselves or may be in denial of their own impurities. Some may even not go through the immersion. So because of the sinful nature of man, once a year at Yom Kippur, the sanctuary needed atonement. In this New Jerusalem, no lying, shameful hypocrites are allowed. HaShem's spirit is "sharper than any double-edged sword, cutting right through to where soul meets spirit and joints meet marrow. It is quick to judge the inner reflections and attitudes of the heart. So before HaShem, nothing created is hidden, but all things are naked and open to the eyes of him to whom we must render an account."[58]

> Next, the angel showed me the river of the water of life, sparkling like crystal, flowing from the throne of God and of the Lamb.[59]

54. Rev 21:25–26
55. Isa 60:11
56. Rev 21:27
57. Acts 2:41; 4:4;
58. Heb 4:12–13
59. Rev 22:1

Yochanan has heard about this river. Is it the river Zechariah spoke of?[60] Or is it that of King David? Or are they the same? He and his companions had often recited, even sang the beautiful tehilla (psalm) King David wrote about it.[61] They often themselves mused on David's prophetic visions. Little did he realize then that one day he would actually see it. The vision reminds him of what he read in the Torah concerning the Garden of Eden.[62]

> Between the main street and the river was the Tree of Life producing twelve kinds of fruit, a different kind every month; and the leaves of the tree were for healing the nations—no longer will there be any curses.[63]

The long-disappeared Tree of Life now stands before him.[64] Its leaves bring healing against the curses brought by the consumption of the fruit of the Tree of the Knowledge of Good and Evil.[65] Since that time, access to the life-giving tree was forbidden and guarded by a mighty cherub.[66]

> The throne of God and of the Lamb will be in the city, and his servants will worship him.[67]

Yochanan had dreamed of the day, the time when he and his brothers will no longer be faced with a human throne and king who requires their "attention." He leaps for joy at the anticipation of that day. Surely, this will encourage his brothers and sisters who daily face privations, torture, and death, for refusing to give worship to a human king and who face punishment for treason, just for wanting to give their worship solely to the King of Kings.

> They will see his face, and his name will be on their foreheads.[68]

60. Zech 14:8
61. Ps 46
62. Gen 2:10
63. Rev 22:2–3
64. Gen 2:9; 3:22
65. Gen 3:6–7
66. Gen 3:24
67. Rev 22:3
68. Rev 22:4

Ya'akov the patriarch saw him face to face. So too was Moshe blessed.[69] Yochanan remembers how Isaiah the prophet taught, "your teacher will no longer hide himself, but with your own eyes you will see your teacher."[70] What a beautiful day it will be when the partial has passed, the perfect has come; when "we see him face to face and know him full as also we have been known."[71] Branded on our forehead with HaShem's seal, our will is fully focused on service to the King.

> Night will no longer exist, so they will need neither the light of a lamp nor the light of the sun, because ADONAI, God, will shine upon them.[72]

"Never again!" Yochanan could exclaim. No more do we know what it is to be absent from the light of the Presence. In that wonderful place, we bask in the primordial Light; the Light of Messiah created on the first day of creation, the first of his ancient works before the earth's beginnings.[73]

> And they will reign as kings forever and ever.[74]

Yochanan was there when Yeshua appointed the twelve as teachers, leaders, and healers. He was also there when, at their return from announcing the Kingdom to the cities of Israel, he told them that they will sit on thrones judging the tribes of Israel. Little did they know that they would also judge the angels. They didn't realize at the time that the Master was establishing them as the new messianic Sanhedrin, to be able to judge matters and establish halacha for the numerous congregations that will arise both in Israel and abroad. The Master was already training them for their future greater responsibilities.

He knew also of Paul, who publicly shamed the Corinthian congregations for improperly filling that legislative roles in their own midst and using unbelievers as judges.[75] The vision is over. Yochanan

69. Gen 32:30; Exod 33:11
70. Isa 30:20
71. 1 Cor 13: 10,12
72. Rev 22:5
73. Gen 1:3–5; Prov 8:22–32
74. Rev 22:5
75. 1 Cor 6:1–6

can't wait to be able to share all this with the disciples. If only he could get out of Patmos and return to his home base of Ephesus. The angel who had poured out the vials and served him as narrator now turns to him.

> Then he said to me, "These words are true and trustworthy: ADONAI, God of the spirits of the prophets, sent his angel to show his servants the things that must happen soon."[76]

Does Yochanan in his Patmos prison have difficulty trusting that all will really be alright? Does he have to pray, asking Yeshua, "I do trust — help my lack of trust!"[77]

> Look! I am coming very soon. Blessed is the person who obeys the words of the prophecy written in this book![78]

Then, Yochanan hears the voice of his dear beloved Master, reassuring him of the imminence of these events. The congregations therefore needed to seriously heed the warnings.

76. Rev 22:6
77. Mk 9:24
78. Rev 22:7

EPILOGUE

> Then I, Yochanan, the one hearing and seeing these things, when I heard and saw them, I fell down to worship at the feet of the angel showing them to me. But he said to me, "Don't do that! I am only a fellow-servant with you and your brothers, the prophets and the people who obey the words in this book. Worship God!"[1]

For a second time, Yochanan is told not to bow before the angelic being speaking to him.[2] He is reminded that we only kneel before the authority of HaShem, not before any angelic or human authority.[3]

> Then he said to me, "Don't seal up the words of the prophecy in this book, because the time of their fulfillment is near."[4]

The prophet Daniel who received a vision as great as that of Yochanan was told to seal the book[5] containing its text, as it pertained to later times. Yochanan, on the other hand, is commanded to not seal the words of his revelation because of the imminence of their fulfillment.

> Whoever keeps acting wickedly, let him go on acting wickedly; whoever is filthy, let him go on being made filthy. Also, whoever is righteous, let him go on doing what is righteous; and whoever is holy, let him go on being made holy. Pay attention! [says Yeshua,] I am coming soon, and my rewards are with me to give to each person according to what he has done.[6]

1. Rev 22:8–9
2. Rev 19:10
3. Est 3:2; Gal 1:8
4. Rev 22:10
5. Dan 12:4
6. Rev 22:11–12

As he hears these frightening words of warning, Yochanan remembers again the ending of Daniel's vision, "but the wicked will keep on acting wickedly, and none of the wicked will understand. But those with discernment will understand."[7]

The faithful shepherd over the Asia Minor communities realizes that there is such a time when the door of repentance is shut; a time when the spirit of rebellion has seized a person beyond healing or cure. The apostle remembers the words of his Master pleading with people that it would be better for them to enter the Kingdom crippled rather than having their whole body thrown into the Gei-Hinnom.[8] He remembers the chill he felt when Yeshua said, "I never knew you! Get away from me, you workers of lawlessness," as he warned people about their own lusts luring them towards counterfeit religious practices.[9]

Yochanan remembers that time on the Mount of Olives just before his Master's execution. They had asked him a question concerning the destruction of the Temple at the end of days. Yeshua then sat by a nearby tree and gave them a long discourse. Though the subject at hand was one of warning and doom, it was also one of joy at the soon coming fulfillment of the promises HaShem made to the fathers.

As he was teaching of these days to come, he taught a parable about virgin bridesmaids who, because they did not have enough oil, were rejected from the marriage banquet,[10] with the chilling words, "Indeed! I tell you, I don't know you!" The Master also taught them that night using a parable about those who did not invest the life the Master gave them into the Kingdom. To those he said, "As for this worthless servant, throw him out in the dark, where people will wail and grind their teeth!"[11]

Finally, he finished his midrash by talking of those who, while knowing the kindness, the altruism, and the generosity of the Master,

7. Dan 12:10
8. Mt 5:27-30
9. Mt 7:21–23
10. Rev 19:7
11. Mt 25:30

lived in selfishness thinking of themselves first and being cold to the needs of others. As he taught the disciples, Yeshua said, "I am the poor, the hungry, the persecuted, and the sick!" "Yes! I tell you that whenever you refused to do it for the least important of these people, you refused to do it for me!' They will go off to eternal punishment, but those who have done what God wants will go to eternal life."[12]

> I am the Aleph and the Tav, the First and the Last, the Beginning and the End. How blessed are those who wash their robes, so that they have the right to eat from the Tree of Life and go through the gates into the city![13]

The Master signs off his oracle with his first introduction. He has overcome the deeds of the evil one. We now have been cleansed enough to inherit the right of return to the Tree of Life; the right of return to Eden. Oh, what a joy; oh, what blessedness!

> Outside are the homosexuals, those involved with the occult and with drugs, the sexually immoral, murderers, idol-worshippers, and everyone who loves and practices falsehood.[14]

One last warning to the Torah disobedient: they will not have entrance in that wonderful city.

> I, Yeshua, have sent my angel to give you this testimony for the Messianic communities. I am the Root and Offspring of David, the bright Morning Star.[15]

Yeshua gives this testimony to Yochanan, not for himself, but for the encouragement of the messianic communities. Does it mean that he will be able to leave Patmos? All his friends who were with him when he was with the Master are now passed on having died for the cause. Yochanan remembers what the Master told Kefa when he asked, "If

12. Mt 24–25
13. Rev 22:13–14)
14. Rev 22:15
15. Rev 22:16

I want him to stay on until I come, what is it to you?"[16] This is more than he expected.

Yes; Yochanan knows that Yeshua is the only rightful Davidic heir to the Jerusalem throne of David. His identifying with the Morning Star gives him more reasons to gaze at the night sky. [17]

> The Spirit and the Bride say, "Come!" Let anyone who hears say, "Come!" And let anyone who is thirsty come — let anyone who wishes, take the water of life free of charge.[18]

Yochanan hears HaShem and the bride call on the people of the world to let go of their own works. They plead for us all to come and quench our thirst at the well of the waters that truly satisfy. He had often read these words from Isaiah at synagogue during Shabbat.[19] He also remembers the words his Master spoke to the woman in Samaria, "whoever drinks the water I will give him will never be thirsty again!"[20] Yochanan knew that he was talking about the living waters of the supernal Torah[21] that the Messiah will give in the World to Come.

> I warn everyone hearing the words of the prophecy in this book that if anyone adds to them, God will add to him the plagues written in this book. And if anyone takes anything away from the words in the book of this prophecy, God will take away his share in the Tree of Life and the holy city, as described in this book.[22]

Yochanan now has the responsibility to convey this message with truth and integrity. He is not allowed to change one word. The words of this

16. Jn 21:22
17. See also 2 Peter 1:19
18. Rev 22:17
19. Isa 55:1
20. Jn 4:13–14
21. Shabbat 88b:7 At the moment when Moses ascended on High, the ministering angels said before the Holy One Blessed Be He: Master of the World, what is one born of a woman doing among us? He said to them: To receive the Torah. The angels said before him: The Torah is a hidden treasure that was concealed for 974 generations before the creation of the world, and you seek to give it to flesh and blood?
22. Rev 22:18–19

oracle are very controversial, even dangerous to him. Not only do they expose the satanic origins of the Roman Empire, but they proclaim the assurance of the demise of its ruthless emperors in favor of him whom they put to death in the cruelest way. These words concur with Moshe as they give us the assurance of the sure return of the children of Jacob to their ancestral God-given land of Israel, from where they were just exiled. In no uncertain terms, these words also proclaim the soon arrival of the ruling Kingdom of God on earth under his Messiah who will remove the Roman-like empires and finally bring true peace, justice, plenty, and freedom for all. Yochanan could already see the new believers from the nations. Certain of them already chafed at the Jewish nature of him who delivered them from the darkness and ignorance of paganism to bring them to the God who made heaven and earth. In their pride and arrogance, they especially rejected the rabbis and sages of Israel. Afraid of persecution, they were attempting to bring Roman religious elements into their congregations. They were even trying to twist the meaning behind the teachings left by Paul, so they would fit their syncretizing efforts. "If they continue in this path, like Jeroboam, they will end up creating a form of cult, which while looking similar, will be far removed from its original. Who knows, they might even become our persecutors!" Yochanan sadly thought to himself. One does not have to change words to change the text. Changing the perspective to a western Roman mindset works just as well! The disciple receives the warning that anyone who does so loses his share in the World to Come. He hopes the future generations will heed that warning!

> The one who is testifying to these things says. "Yes, I am coming soon!" Amen! Come, Lord Yeshua! May the grace of the Lord Yeshua be with all![23]

23. Rev 22:20–21

MEET RABBI GAVRIEL LUMBROSO

Gavriel Lumbroso was born in Paris, France, a descendent of a long line of the Lumbroso family who have an extensive Jewish history. He was a dedicated member of Zionist Youth Groups in France from an early age leading up to the time of his Bar Mitzvah at the Wailing Wall in Jerusalem. Eventually Patrick made "*aliyah*" as a young teen where he did his studies at an Ulpan farm/school for young immigrants.

Still seeking, he befriended a young man on a trip to Europe who shared Isaiah 53 with him and taught him about Messiah. This was a turning point on his spiritual journey for Yeshua (Jesus).

Gavriel met and married his wife, Christina, while in France, and they spent years abroad in Christian outreach from Eastern Europe to S.E. Asia. They have six grown children. Gavriel and his wife presently reside in the USA.

In addition to running a Torah study group in Oregon and spending much of his time teaching the Hebrew roots of Christian faith, he also teaches French, Hebrew, History, Geography, and current events to teens in home-school groups, and private Christian schools. He and his wife also compose and play in their Messianic/Israeli music band called, "The Lumbrosos," and have produced three CDs.

Patrick is a chaplain supervisor for the Estacada fire department in Oregon and an ordained Rabbi under the United Messianic Jewish Assembly.

GLOSSARY

Acharet-Hayamim	The end of days, or the endtime.
ADONAI	The LORD
Aleph	The first letter of the Hebrew alphabet
Bavel	Babylon
Besora	The Good News/the Gospel
Betula	Virgin
Chesed	Covenant keeping devotion and loyalty; commonly translated as 'grace'
Cohen/Cohanim	Priest/Priests
Eliyahu	Elijah
Diaspora	Exile
Gan-Eden	The garden HaShem created east of Eden at the time of creation
Gei-Hinnom	Gehenna
Halacha	Spiritual walk; personal religious observance application
HaSatan	The Adversary; the Devil
HaShem	A Hebrew circumlocution for the Ineffable name of God.
Havdala	Short home ceremony at the closing of the Shabbat

Kadosh	Holy/Sanctified
Kosher	Biblically fit for consumption
Kefa	Peter
Kiddush	Sabbath sanctification prayer
Kiddush HaShem	The act of dying as a martyr to the faith
Korban/ Korbanot	Altar offering
Lukas	Luke
Mashiach	Messiah/Christ
Mazzaroth	The twelve constellations that make up the Zodiac
Menorah	Temple candelabrum
Midrash	A commentary, often in the form of a parable, to a biblical text.
Moshe	Moses
Neshser	Vulture/eagle
Olam hazeh	This present world or age
Or	Light
Pidyon Haben	Dedication of the first-born
Rome	Rome
Ruach Hakodesh	The Holy Spirit of God
Shaliach	Emissary; apostle
Shavuot	The festival of Weeks; Pentecost
Sheker-mashiach	Anti-christ

Shim'on	Simon/Simeon
Shlomo	Solomon
Shofar	Ceremonial rams horn
Sukkot	The Feast of Tabernacles
Tahor	Ritually sanctified
Talmid/talmidim	Disciple/disciples
Talmud	Body of Jewish Bible commentaries starting from when they began to appear in written form in the second century C.E.
Tamei	Ritually contaminated
Tamid	Name for the twice daily Temple offering.
Tanakh	Hebrew acronym standing for "Torah; Nevi'im (prophets); K'tuvim (writings), and is used to refer to the Old Testament of the Bible.
Tanin	Sea-monster or beast/crocodile
Targum	The Tanakh in Aramaic translation
Tav	The last letter of the Hebrew alphabet
Tephilin	Payer boxes Jewish people wrap on their arms and head
Teshuvah	Repentance
Tzaddik	A righteous person
Tzaddik Hador	The righteous one for a certain generation

Vayikrah	"And he called…" Leviticus
Yerushalayim	Jerusalem
Yeshua	Hebrew for "Savior," Jesus in Greek
Ya'akov	Jacob
Ya'akov HaTsaddik	James the Just
Yochanan	John (the disciple of Yeshua)
Yochanan HaMatvil	John the Immerser
Yom Kippur	The Day of Atonement
Yom Teruah	Rosh Hashana

BIBLIOGRAPHY

Aggadic Midrash. Seder Olam Rabah. Midrash Rabah/Shir ha-Shirim Rabbah 7. https://www.sefaria.org/Seder_Olam_Rabbah?lang=bi

Ben Maimon, Moses (also known as Maimonides and referred to by the acronym Rambam). Mishneh Torah, Bet HaMikdash 6:11.

Charles, R. H. (Translator). The Book of Enoch. http://www.sacred-texts.com/bib/boe/boe004.html. 1917. The Book of the Apocalypse of Baruch (translated from the Syriac). Wipf & Stock Publishers. Eugene, Oregon.

Eiseman, Rabbi. The Book of Ezekiel. Artscroll Mesorah Publications. 1989.

Eusebius. The History of the Church from Christ to Constantine. Translator. G.A. Williamson.

Foxe, John. Foxe's Book of Martyrs. Bridge-Logos Publishers. 2001.

Grote, Georges. Conquests of Cyrus the Great. Createspace Independent Publishing Platform. 2016.

Jewish Virtual Library, a project of AICE (Advanced International Certificate of Education). Ancient Jewish History, retrieved from, http://www.jewishvirtuallibrary.org/the-menorah.

Josephus, Flavius. Antiquities of the Jews. New Updated edition. Hendrickson Publishers. 2000.

Klein, John and Adam Spears. Lost in Translation Vol 2. Covenant Research Institute. 2009.

Lancaster, D. T. Torah Club 3. Voice of the Prophets. First Fruits of Zion. 2009.

Luzzato, Rabbi Moshe Chayim. Derech HaShem. Feldheim. 2009.

Shick, Eleazer Shlomo. A Voice Calls Out to G'd. Chapter 19 on Zohar Leviticus 20a. CreateSpace, 1987.

Stern, David H. The Complete Jewish Bible for E-Sword. B0009. Messianic Jewish Publishers.

The Babylonian Talmud (Talmud Bavli):Tractate Rosh Hashana; Nedarim/ Tractate Mo'ed Katan 28a/Tractate Sotah 5/Sanhedrin 98a/Tractate Pesachim/Tractate Chagigah/Tractate Shabbat. http://www.jewishvirtuallibrary.org/babylonian-talmud-full-text.

The Seventh Haftara of Comfort. Shemot Rabbah 2:5. https://www.sefaria.org/Shemot_Rabbah.2?lang=bi.

Tauber, Yanki. Based on the teachings of the Lubavitcher Rebbe, Rabbi Menachem Mendel Schneerson concerning The Shabbat of Vison. http://www.chabad.org/library/article_cdo/aid/52985/jewish/Shabbat-of-Vision.htm/Or HaTorah LeNach, Vol. II, p. 234./ Reshimos HaTzemach Tzedek LeEichah. fn. to p. 45.

Printed in the United States
by Baker & Taylor Publisher Services